Table of Contents

C000055617

To Alex and Frank, thanks for all your help :) k

Acknowledgments

Some of the most exciting features of Microsoft Office 2003 involve enhancing collaboration and improving communication, and the team who worked on this book exemplifies the best of those concepts. (We used SharePoint Team Services to work collaboratively from very different areas of the world, by the way.) Huge thanks go to each of the following people for the part they played in getting this book into your hands:

- Kristen Weatherby, project editor, for somehow moving this project through at break-neck speed while ensuring its quality and keeping her cool;

- Alex Blanton, acquisitions editor, for thinking this book was possible in the first place and then gracefully removing all the stumbling blocks that fell into our path;

- Claudette Moore, my agent at Moore Literary Agency, for being a great sounding board and taking care of business details so that I could keep writing;

- Brian Johnson, technical editor at Microsoft Press and the author of Chapter 7, who jumped in at almost the last minute and wrote a wonderful chapter (and helped capture images);

- W. Frederick Zimmerman, who did a terrific job explaining the exciting new features of Microsoft Office OneNote 2003 in Chapter 4, which he contributed;

- Steve Sagman proprietor of Studioserv, for his always stellar hands-on management of this project; Teri Kieffer for a great—and fast—copy edit; Sharon Bell for her artistic FrameMaker talents; and Julie Kawabata for a fine index.

Finally, I truly appreciate the help of the many people inside and outside Microsoft who answered questions, provided support documents, and offered examples and insights I've used in this book. Special thanks to authors Jim Buyens, Mark Dodge, Craig Stinson, Acey Bunch, and Michael Young, as well as Microsoft professionals Roan Kang and Frank Rice. Your contributions have made this a better book.

Introduction

A First Look at Microsoft Office 2003

Welcome to *First Look Microsoft Office 2003*. This book introduces you to the new, far-reaching features of Microsoft Office 2003 and shows how you can put them to work in your business, organization, or home. If you work with ideas—and we all do, in one way or another—your imagination will kick into high gear as you see how Office 2003 can support the total lifespan of an idea, from that first scribble on the back of your business card, to the final Web publication produced by your management team, and the translation and distribution of the smart document to your satellite offices in 14 countries around the globe.

You don't have to be part of a large organization to get maximum benefit from the new features in Office. Employees of small to mid-size businesses, entrepreneurs, and independent contractors—anyone who exchanges ideas and data with someone else—will find features in Office that enhance communication and collaboration; make project management simpler than ever; capture innovative ideas from everyone on the team; and easily produce and change documents, Web pages, reports, and presentations based on data saved in structured formats. It's the "create-it-once, use-it-many-times" idea, which allows you to work smarter and faster by streamlining the creation process and reducing the margin for error among different versions of the same document.

Answering the Big Questions

As you are considering whether to upgrade your existing Office software to the new release—or perhaps whether to invest in Office for the first time—you may find yourself wrestling with the same questions many organizations ask:

■ Is the new release worth my investment of time, money, and training?

■ How will it affect the way I do business?

■ Will the new features really make a difference for the work I do every day?

■ How hard will the new features be to implement and use?

■ Is this the version I should upgrade to, or should I wait for the next one?

First Look Microsoft Office 2003 helps you answer those questions by detailing the key features in such a way that you'll be able to see yourself using them. You'll learn about new features and understand how existing features have been enhanced. You'll see how the seamless integration of the applications with the functionality and resources of the Internet make collaboration easier than ever before. And you'll discover why Office 2003 represents a major shift in the way businesses can leverage the knowledge they already have to be more in tune and competitive in today's fast-paced, information-hungry market.

Who Is This Book For?

First Look Microsoft Office 2003 is for people who want to know the ins and outs of the latest release of Microsoft Office. This could include anyone, but the information here will be most interesting to people in these general categories:

■ Knowledge workers who are looking for a better, smarter way to capture and use data

■ Business professionals who are responsible for making decisions about purchasing and deploying company software

■ IT specialists who set and maintain software standards for their companies

- Small business owners who are looking for applications that support the latest data and communication technologies

- Independent professionals who work as part of remote teams and collaboratively create end products

- Solution developers interested in knowing more about the new Office to see how they can enhance or augment existing features by developing third-party products or services

Of course, if you're simply an Office enthusiast interested in knowing more about the capabilities of this new version, this book will serve you, too! No matter which group you belong to, you'll find many interesting ideas and possibilities here that will spark your imagination and inspire you to try new things with Office 2003.

What You'll Find in This Book

The primary goal of this book is to shine a light on the many new and enhanced features of Office 2003 and show you how you might apply them in your own business, organization, or home. We've tried to tame the massive amount of information available and distill it to help you:

- Learn more about the various new and enhanced features of Office 2003

- Get ideas for the ways you'll be able to put Office 2003 to work

- Grasp how you can capture more ideas instantly, apply them immediately and share them with others

- Explore ways you can communicate more efficiently and effectively

- See how you can use the Office 2003 features to integrate all the applications with the resources and functionality of the Web

- Understand how support for XML allows you to take your data farther by producing results in a variety of forms

- Find out how Office 2003 features can help you streamline collaboration and share data, while maintaining a secure environment

What You Won't Find Here

Because this book focuses on giving you a "first look" at the new version of Office yourself, we don't spend a lot of time giving you a blow-by-blow tutorial in each of the different feature areas. Instead, you'll find a good, solid introduction to the new-and-improved features of Office 2003, examples of how the various aspects of the program can be applied (in businesses of varying sizes), and suggestions for the quickest and easiest ways to put the enhancements to use in your day-to-day work.

Inside This Book

This book is divided into eight chapters, each focusing on a different aspect of Office 2003.

Chapter 1, "An Overview of Microsoft Office 2003," gives you a sense of the overall vision of Office 2003 and touches on key features that are common to each of the core applications.

Chapter 2, "Microsoft Office Outlook 2003 and Messaging," explores the new additions and changes in Microsoft Outlook and examines the integration of instant messaging throughout Office.

Chapter 3, "Collaborating Using SharePoint Team Services and SharePoint Portal Server," shows you how you can collaborate more effectively and efficiently than ever before with the many added and enhanced features of SharePoint Team Services V2.

Chapter 4, "Introduction to Microsoft Office OneNote 2003," highlights this new idea-management tool that can be used with standard computers, Pocket PCs, and Tablet PCs.

Chapter 5, "Support for XML," looks closely at the ways in which you'll now be able to work with XML in Word, Excel, and Access.

Chapter 6, "XML Applied: Smart Documents, Smart Tags, and Microsoft Office InfoPath 2003," shows how you can create and use Microsoft InfoPath to gather data that can then be stored independently and used in a variety of forms you control.

Chapter 7, "Upgrading, Deploying, and Administering Office 2003," discusses the new, easier-to-use deployment features so that you can get a glimpse of how easy upgrading to the new Office will be.

Chapter 8, "Microsoft Office 2003 Productivity Enhancements," gives you an overview of all the enhanced features in each of the core applications that allow you to streamline your efforts and increase productivity.

A "Resources" section at the end of the book provides you with current links to additional sites and documents where you can find updates about Office 2003.

Navigation Elements

First Look Microsoft Office 2003 uses a few special elements to call your attention to additional information you might find helpful:

■ Tips give you suggestions for ways you can use a specific feature or service.

■ Notes provide information complementary to the discussion at hand.

■ More Info readeraids

■ Cross-references point out additional references you can consult for further information.

Now that you know the general lay of the land, you're probably prepared to get that first look at Microsoft Office 2003. If you're ready, turn the page and let's get started.

1

An Overview of Microsoft Office 2003

Information workers dream of programs as flexible as humans are, powerful enough to capture, process, and produce information in a variety of forms, yet simple enough to master quickly. Seamlessly integrating these applications with intranet and Internet resources so that you can find what you need when you need it and apply it almost instantly is part and parcel of this dream.

The last few years have taught us that our simple, interpersonal communication is as powerful and packed with information as the reports and analyses we labor over. We've also learned that working in groups brings far greater benefit in terms of creativity, vision, specialization, and error-trapping than does working alone within our office walls. Physical distance no longer limits us, given virtual meeting rooms, online conferences, instant messaging, and collaborative scheduling. We don't have to run down the hall to check a fact because we can ping a colleague using instant messaging—right now.

"What's possible" has been stretched to include faster, more efficient, further-reaching, and more flexible rules about how we complete our work. Our quickly evolving understanding of what's possible at work drives the need for faster, more flexible, and more efficient tools to get the job done. That's where Microsoft Office 2003 comes in.

Why? Because You Can[1]

You can carry around thousands of songs in a pocket-sized device. You can watch any U.S. TV show on your home computer anywhere in the world. You can read the diaries of hundreds of thousands of people. You can make a call from the road anytime, anywhere. You can fly thousands of miles for a few dozen dollars or euros. You can order any book, CD, or video directly from your desk and consume it right there without having to get up out of your chair. You can find out almost everything about almost anything within seconds. You can send a photograph to loved ones in a second. You can travel to almost any location in the world within less than 24 hours. You can subscribe to have black socks delivered to you every quarter. You can start a company with a few people all from their desks; no garage necessary. You can write a book, offer it online for free, and still make money. You can sell your attic junk for ridiculous money. You can enjoy life.

Welcome to another week in the 21st century.

The Challenges Information Workers Face

The worldwide community of Office users totals more than 300 million people (now *that's* a big family!), and the needs and wishes of the audience are as diverse as the countries and industries they live and work in. Their experience levels range from novice to advanced user to developer/expert. Some users would choose speed over power. Others want greater flexibility with third-party products. Still others would like the new Office to be more secure, more stable, or more streamlined in one area or another. All want easier access to information, the ability to smoothly apply data across the range of applications, and processes and procedures that can be personalized to provide solutions for their own unique work challenges.

---

1. Adapted from a posting by Stefan Smalla, on Stefan Smalla's Info Feed: Weblog on business, technology, startups, and some more *www.smalla.net/infofeed/2003/01/19/why_because_you_can.shtml*. Used with permission.

Office 2003 is designed specifically to meet the biggest hurdles that people who work with information typically face:

- **Information Fatigue.**   We deal with lots of data—from reports and Web sites to meetings and phone calls. We listen to presentations, watch television, hear Web broadcasts, and go to seminars. We receive thousands of e-mails per week, subscribe to online news-letters, and visit discussions and newsgroups. Information flies at us from all directions at all times, in a huge array of forms. How do we sift through the glut of data we absorb and keep only what is useful for our particular job, team, or company? The tools in Office 2003 for grabbing notes, recording ideas, and sharing thoughts instantly enable you to get hold of and act on ideas as they occur, reducing their chances of being buried in a virtual pile of not-so-important reading.

- **Inefficient collaboration.**   The idea of workgroups is terrific, but it often requires a long evolution. How many people worked on your last annual report? Who managed the process? How many hours did your manager spend trying to find suitable meeting times and places? Did using a team approach save you time or cost you more? The new Office 2003 includes important enhancements for working collaboratively, including a new meeting workspace service that helps you organize and facilitate meetings online.

- **Disconnected islands of data.**   Does this sound like your office? Imagine that Accounting prepared a document last spring that described each of the products in your 2002 line, breaking down the costs according to your various departments. As you prepare your proposal for the three new products you want to introduce in 2004, you find that the document was created in Word but was not part of an Excel spreadsheet, which means that when a manager corrected the amounts later in the year, the new totals were never updated. So you have a choice: You can use the previously corrected document and make the cost corrections by hand, or you can use the Excel spreadsheet with the correct values (but not the cost-center calcula-tions you want), and re-create the information you need. What a lot of work! Office 2003 helps you use your data more efficiently by pro-viding Smart Documents, collaboration with Microsoft Office InfoPath 2003, improved smart tags, and increased support for XML, which enables you to store your data independent of its form and use it to produce a variety of end results.

- **Lack of business process integration.** Even in the smoothest-running businesses, a lot of overlap occurs in business process. One department replicates what another department is doing at the other end of the building. With enhanced collaboration features and improved support for XML, Office 2003 can help you cut down on duplication of effort and allow all departments to share access to information that would support each of their efforts in unique ways.

- **Outdated and upgraded systems disconnect the usefulness of data.** As businesses change and grow, their systems also change and grow. Most large organizations go through elaborate—and expensive—upgrade processes to ensure that important data migrates from generation to generation. But in many organizations, some data is simply left unusable in today's applications—and workers re-key existing information or scan piles of printouts to transfer information from old legacy systems to today's servers. Office 2003 integrates into the core applications industry-standard Extensible Markup Language (XML), allowing organizations to store, access, and publish data from almost any system in an unlimited number of forms.

- **Underutilization of productivity tools.** The core applications in Office are so feature-laden that many businesses don't use them fully; people tend to perform a specific number of tasks with each program without a sense of how the programs could work together to improve and accelerate business processes. Office 2003 increases productivity in each of the core applications—Word, Excel, Outlook, Access, and FrontPage—and enhances the easy way the applications work together to make you more productive and efficient.

- **Lack of true mobility.** Many of today's information workers work on the move. They travel to meet clients; they make business calls on cell phones in the airport; they meet in coffee shops and gyms as well as boardrooms, courtrooms, and classrooms. As a people on the go, information workers need flexible ways to gather the ideas and information they encounter along the way. Laptop computers provide one way to capture information on the run, but even the smallest laptops can be more trouble than they're worth in a fast-paced brainstorming meeting. Office 2003's support for input from mobile devices—including the new Tablet PC with enhanced Ink support—gives mobile users yet another way to capture and use important in-the-moment information.

- **Concern for security and integrity of data.**   One of the obstacles to easy collaboration and document sharing (two key components in effective teamwork) has been concern for the protection of proprietary data. How do you control the distribution and modification of proprietary documents in your organization? In Office 2003, Microsoft introduces Information Rights Management, a feature that enables you to protect your information by controlling what others can do with it.

Any new release of a software product will fix what fell short in the previous version, but Office 2003 brings much more to the table than corrective measures. Although Office 2003 *does* improve Outlook clunkiness, increase stability, and beef up security, the exciting innovations in Office 2003 are likely to inspire you to take a closer look. Whatever your particular obstacles might be right now—communication dead ends, repetition of effort, security holes, underuse of existing data and processes, workgroup struggles, or something else—Office 2003 can solve them. In the next section, you'll see how this version of Office is a new, highly flexible, and fast platform that enables you to capture information instantly, share ideas easily, work with data efficiently, and produce results in a variety of forms that fit the tasks you want to accomplish.

The Office 2003 Answer

Office 2003 is designed to support the entire life cycle of an idea—from that first spark in the back of your head to the brainstorming meeting with Product Development to the project management and final production of the end result. Each aspect of Office—the core applications, online services, customizability of key features, instant communication, and underlying XML support—provides ways to capture, explore, contribute, and build on your ideas. With an emphasis on communication and collaboration, the vision for Office 2003 includes these important aspects of working with information effectively:

- **Capturing ideas wherever and whenever they spring up.** Support for the Tablet PC in all core applications lets you jot notes on your Tablet (or on your Pocket PC) in a meeting and then e-mail them directly to team members; you can save, store, and file information in a variety of ways, including as XML, which gives you the ability to pull it into an almost unlimited number of forms.

■ **Communicating instantly with integrated messaging.** Windows Messenger is now built right into Microsoft Office Outlook 2003 (and appears as smart tags when you type recognized names in application documents), which means you can see whether others on your contact list are online. If they are, you can ask a quick question or send a fast update while you're thinking about it.

■ **Collaborating more effectively with enhanced team features.** Improved collaboration features in the major applications as well as improvements in SharePoint Team Services make working with others both inside and outside your organization easier to manage than ever. Using new meeting and document workspaces, you can gather and discuss (and revise) anywhere you have access to the Web; you can also customize templates for your SharePoint site, compare calendars, set alerts, and create customized lists for the way you organize and view your site.

■ **Creating a personalized collection of services you need and want.** The new MyOffice site, available only to Office users, is an online collection of supports and services that help you answer questions about Office *and* extend its core functionality through complementary products and services that facilitate your work process—in the best way for you.

■ **Making your data go further with XML.** XML (Extensible Markup Language) has changed the way we work with information by separating the data—the document's structure and meaning—from its format (Microsoft Office Word 2003 document, Microsoft Office Excel 2003 spreadsheet, Microsoft Office FrontPage 2003 Web site, and so on). Because the data is stored separately using a structured, self-describing language, the data itself can be used in different forms to produce a variety of end results. This allows you to use the same data to create a brochure, a Web site, a PivotTable, a Microsoft Office Access 2003 report, and so on. You save time creating what you *want* to create instead of copying existing documents, removing formats, and starting over. Smart Documents use XML to bring this enhanced functionality to Word and Excel, and InfoPath enable you to prepare sophisticated forms to gather and reuse information.

■ **Simplifying the upgrade and deployment process.** Adding new software always involves a learning curve and, depending on the size and structure of your organization, can be a major undertaking. Office 2003 takes a shot at resolving upgrade challenges by adding a new Custom Installation Wizard and Custom Maintenance Wizard for corporate deployment. For individual users, the Setup interface and process have been improved, stabilized, and expanded to be more accessible for all users.

■ **Protecting valuable business information with IRM.** Information Rights Management features enable you to grant or restrict the ability to print, forward, edit, and copy documents. This ensures the integrity of your intellectual property and allows you to grant permissions to selected people rather than making it available to all who have access to your system.

Throughout the rest of this chapter, we'll look more specifically at how Office 2003 meets the needs of individual information workers and small and large organizations by offering new and improved products and services that make communication, collaboration, and data application easier and more flexible.

What's New in Office 2003?

With a focus on connecting people, processes, and information, Office 2003 is flexible enough to enable you to capture ideas in whatever form they occur, use them to create documents (including spreadsheets, reports, e-mail messages, Web pages, and more) individually or as part of a group, and save them in such a way that they can be ported to all kinds of different products. Put simply, the new features let you gather data more easily, work with it more efficiently, and save it so as to prevent more work later.

This section gives you a bird's-eye view of the new features in Office 2003. For more in-depth coverage, see the chapters related to the topic you're most interested in exploring.

Office 2003: Top 12 Things You Need to Know

1. This version of Office has a greater number of features and more support for collaboration than past Office releases.

2. The Office interface now uses Microsoft Windows XP themes, so users can rely even more on consistency between programs.

3. Office 2003 includes Outlook additions and enhancements that make communication easier, faster, smarter, and more secure.

4. SharePoint Team Services use Microsoft Windows Server 2003 to give you a cutting-edge, secure, collaborative team option you can use from any Web access point.

5. Office 2003 takes a huge step toward extending the usefulness of data with full support for XML in Word, Excel, and Access.

6. Smart Documents, smart tags, and InfoPath enable you to create intelligent documents that are easier to work with, and to save data in a secure, structured form that can be applied in unlimited ways.

7. Seamless integration of support for Office on Microsoft.com enables users to broaden their resources with a click of the mouse; access to training, upgrades, solutions, and services are available on the site.

8. The new Microsoft Office OneNote 2003 tool allows you to capture thoughts on the fly in your own handwriting (or in doodles, recorded audio, and more) and port them to applications as usable data.

9. Improved customer service channels help keep Office 2003 customers in touch with Microsoft and one another.

10. Enhanced security features and improved setup make upgrading, deploying, and maintaining Office easier.

11. Information Rights Management (IRM) enables you to control who has access to your proprietary documents and limit the tasks (copying, forwarding, printing, and more) that anyone can perform.

12. Many new features in the core applications make "living in Office" a more pleasant, efficient, and productive experience.

Improvements in Setup

One of the most noticeable changes in Office 2003 is its simplified installation. Gone are the glitches and hitches of earlier versions, and because Office doesn't modify the system files, you don't have to reboot after installation is complete. Office gives you the choice of creating a local cache for installation files, which enables you to repair, install on first use, and update Office later without using the CD. In a corporate environment, the new Custom Installation Wizard will step you easily through the setup process.

Changes in the Office 2003 User Interface

The next obvious change in Office 2003 is its look and feel. Office now sports a more "sophisticated" look, following the color schemes and element designs in Windows XP. You'll notice a similar theme right from first use—a "pipe" effect and gradient colors in the task panes and menus; changes in the menu options and task panes. (See Figure 1-1.)

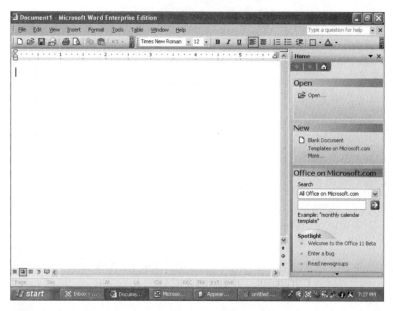

Figure 1-1   The new Office 2003 interface has a more sophisticated look that follows Windows XP themes.

After considerable research, the Office team went with this new look because so many users "spend all day in Office," and experienced users want a more polished look. The task panes have been enhanced to show subheadings on a second color bar, making it easy to see at a glance where one grouping of commands ends and the next begins.

Some of the individual applications include significant interface changes as well. In Outlook, for example, you'll find a three-column view that lets you preview an e-mail message without scrolling. (See Figure 1-2.) An instant-message preview also pops up, showing the first few words of each incoming e-mail message so that you can see what's coming in without interrupting your current task or even taking your hands off the keyboard.

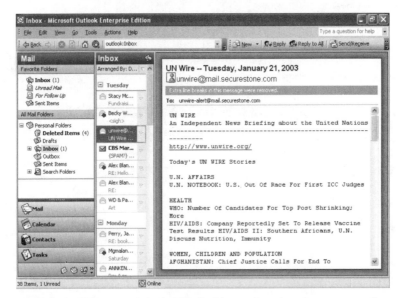

Figure 1-2   You can customize Outlook's new interface to rearrange the column format.

Seamless Integration with Office on Microsoft.com

Another big change in both the look and feel and the functionality of Office is increased integration with Office on Microsoft.com. Links to Office resources are no longer buried in the Help menu as Office on the Web; now you can link to information online (including Thesaurus, Encarta, and more) right in the task pane in each of the core Office applications. (See Figure 1-3, on the next page.)

Figure 1-3 You can access Help from both your local system and the resources available on Microsoft.com.

The entire help system in Office 2003 has been extended beyond individual workstations. If you are connected to the Internet when you choose a help topic or enter a word or phrase in the Ask-A-Question box at the top of individual Office applications, the Help system displays not only the help information on your local (or networked) system, but also brings to the Help window information from microsoft.com (including Knowledgebase articles) that can give you the most current information on the topic you need help with, as well as links to additional resources.

Office on Microsoft.com is more than just how-to articles and help resources. The new site has the same look and feel as the rest of Office 2003 and offers a number of new features, including these:

From the Experts

Mark Dodge, co-author of *Microsoft Office Excel 2003 Inside Out* had this to say about the new, improved Office 2003 Help system: "Having this sort of live connection with help content on the Web makes it more stable, more up-to-date, and more likely that you're going to get a lot better information—more accurate than you've ever had before." He adds that the revised help and enhanced integration with Office on Microsoft.com will help employers save time and money while providing a way for employees to find fast answers and continued online training.

- The Assistance Center Web page for Office on Microsoft.com provides a'nsticles that help you find answers to common questions, explore key features in each of the programs, look for specific help in newsgroups, or report a problem.

- Office Online Training offers online classes, Web-based interactive training, and self-paced exercises. In the Training section, you'll find some specific task-oriented projects to help you accomplish a particular goal (for example, create a baby growth chart, a party guest list, or a for-sale sign), more general application-oriented introductions (create an outline in Word or use Excel as a calculator), or explore online courses in each of the primary office applications (Word, Outlook, Excel, FrontPage, Access, and Microsoft Office PowerPoint 2003).

- A Templates link is available on the Home and New task panes in each application. Clicking the Templates link takes you to a Template Gallery with dozens of professionally designed templates for common business and personal uses. (See Figure 1-4.)

Figure 1-4 An online Template Gallery, available in the task pane through the link to Office on Microsoft.com, offers dozens of document templates for download.

- The Clip Art and Media link in the Office on Microsoft.com site allows you to download thousands of pieces of clip art and animations for use in your documents or business (or fun) presentations.

- Office Update gives you the latest on Office and lets you know when new information is available.

- In the "Things to Do" area of Office on Microsoft.com, you'll notice enhancements in the feedback loop. Now you can report a problem online or even suggest new content for the site.

- Office Marketplace offers Web services that complement Office 2003. For example, you might use Marketplace to find someone to convert your PDF files to Word documents, translate your German reports into English, or find an online fax service. Marketplace is open to third-party vendors offering Office-related products and services.

A Farther Reach for Research

The Research task pane (available in the Tools menu) enables you to search online references to do research. If you frequently search scientific journals, grantmaking announcements, academic writings, or any number of other online sources, you can add them to your research options and perform the search easily in the Research task pane. (See Figure 1-5.)

Figure 1-5   The Research task pane extends your research options by scouring the online resources you select.

Capturing Ideas as They Occur

If your work relies on good note-taking, the new OneNote application can make your professional life a lot easier. OneNote enables you to capture, store, organize, and use the notes you create; no more retyping text from wrinkled napkins and the backs of envelopes. If you've got OneNote on a Tablet PC, a Pocket PC, or your regular work computer (with a writing-pad peripheral), you can write, draw, or speak your notes as you make them, and OneNote timestamps and saves the information for you automatically. Once you capture the notes, you can organize, use, and share them as needed—whether as an audio clip of catch phrases for your newest product, a diagram showing the potential restructuring of your business, a quick bit of conversation with a developer you just met, or a followup task list for your team.

OneNote is exciting because it works the way you do, enabling you to grab those good ideas that can lose their sparkle (or disappear altogether) when you try to recall your inspiration later.

> **More Info** For a more in-depth look at OneNote, including the philosophy behind its development and examples of how you can use it at work or home, see Chapter 4, "Introduction to Microsoft Office OneNote 2003."

Another addition that fits in the "capturing information" category is the introduction of the Microsoft Business Contact Manager. This application is included with Office 2003 and allows owners of small businesses and entrepreneurs to capture and organize crucial information on leads, contacts, and events. The Business Contact Manager enables users to manage customer information and relationships in one common utility, import information from other contact managers (such as ACT!), and use data tables and lists from program like Excel and QuickBooks.

> **More Info** For more about the Business Contact Manager, see Chapter 8, "Microsoft Office 2003 Productivity Enhancements."

Enhanced Collaboration with SharePoint Team Services

SharePoint Team Services is a Web service that enables teams and workgroups to collaborate more easily. Access to SharePoint Team Services is built into FrontPage, from which users can create simple or customized SharePoint pages by selecting a wizard and walking through the process. A SharePoint Team Services site helps teams get organized, communicate with each other, schedule events, and collaborate on documents.

SharePoint Team Services, first introduced in Office XP, has been significantly enhanced in Office 2003 to let users put document workspace templates to work, making document collaboration easier. The Shared Workspace functionality is built right into Word's Tools menu, so users can move seamlessly to the shared space without ever leaving Word. The new Meeting Workspace feature creates a repository for meeting-related information that is maintained in a secure, team-accessible space, and allows meetings to be scheduled and hosted online. (See Figure 1-6.) Other enhancements in SharePoint Team Services make it easier to customize sites and add new list and field types for more complete data management.

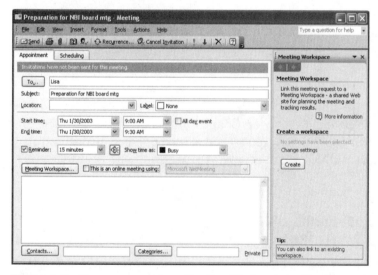

Figure 1-6   Users can create a Meeting Workspace when they set up a meeting in Outlook.

> **More Info**   For more information on SharePoint Team Services and the impact the services can have on the way business teams collaborate, see Chapter 3, "Collaborating Using SharePoint Team Services and SharePoint Portal Server."

Extending Data Functionality with XML

XML (Extensible Markup Language) is a new language standard that enables businesses, individuals, and developers to create documents in which data is stored independently of the form in which it is presented. This means, for example, that the data in an XML document is stored as one set of information, and the format of the data (how it appears) is stored separately. Because the data is self-describing, it can be used in other types of documents (reports, letters, databases, spreadsheets, and Web pages, for example) without having to be retyped or laboriously copied, reformatted, or applied as needed in another form.

Although XML support was a limited feature in Office XP, it is fully supported in Office 2003 through Word, Excel, and Access, with features and help that enable users to take advantage of XML using existing or customized schemas.

> **More Info**   For a closer look at XML and its possible applications throughout Office, see Chapter 5, "Support for XML," and Chapter 8, "Microsoft Office 2003 Productivity Enhancements," which go into specific XML features in Word, Excel, and Access.

Making Your Documents Smarter with Smart Documents, InfoPath, and Enhanced Smart Tags

What would you call a document that can arrive via e-mail or Web download, do its own security checks upon being opened, and offer users or readers contextual help in the task pane while they review or modify it? Office 2003 smart documents are built on XML schemas that allow developers to create customized documents with contextual help, context-sensitive prompts, content suggestions, data lists, or links to additional resources. Smart documents are supported in Word, Excel, and PowerPoint; they take interactive, specialized document creation and application to a new level.

Smart tags, introduced in Office XP, have been enhanced in Office 2003. Now developers can create more powerful smart tags with a larger range of actions and applicability. Smart tags are now available in PowerPoint and Access for the first time, and developers can create smart tags with cascading menus, giving users a greater range of choice and developers more room for customization.

InfoPath is a new offering that enables businesses and individuals to really apply the power of XML. On the front end, InfoPath look like highly interactive, customized forms with contextual prompts; on the back end, InfoPath are highly structured XML documents that gather the entered data for reuse and reapplication in an unlimited number of ways. InfoPath comes with sample forms that can be used as is or modified to specific business uses. They also include forms for developers that illustrate the various ways InfoPath can be designed to fit into existing business procedures.

> **More Info**   Chapter 6, "XML Applied: Smart Documents, Smart Tags, and Microsoft Office InfoPath 2003," goes into the key features in Microsoft Office 2003 that will put a sparkle in any developer's eye. Learn about the new, customizable XML-based features that enable you to create task panes tailored to your business needs; extend the functionality and reach of smart tags; and develop sophisticated, highly interactive, and structured forms with InfoPath.

Improvements in Office 2003 Security

Enhancing collaboration and sharing ideas and projects are great ways to increase productivity and creativity, but they're risky, so security is an important component of Office 2003. Many security-related improvements built into the infrastructure of Office and its core applications are transparent to the user. Internet Explorer and Office 2003 now share the same trusted certificate list— making it easier for you to manage accepted sites—and Office 2003 has improved compatibility with third-party anti-virus software.

New IRM Technology

A new addition in Office 2003, Information Rights Management (IRM) technology runs on Windows Server (with a premium Client Access License) to give organizations running Office 2003 and SharePoint Team Services V2 the ability to limit access and editability of key documents. With IRM, users and managers can restrict functions that enable documents to be copied or forwarded outside an organization; additionally, range-based permissions and expiration dates can be used to limit and terminate access.

IRM is designed to help you safeguard the valuable information in your organization and works alongside your current policies for security, document confidentiality, and e-mail use. For more about working with IRM in the various Office applications, see Chapter 8, "Microsoft Office 2003 Productivity Enhancements."

Productivity Improvements

Many of the big changes in Office 2003 have to do with communication and collaboration, but each of the core applications has seen improvements of its own as well. The biggest changes in Word involve the behind-the-schemes functionality of XML, the connectivity enhancements of the Research task pane, and the integration with Office on Microsoft.com. You'll see and use other new features, too, such as the new Reading Layout and the ability to mark documents as read-only, which lets you control access to and modification of important documents. Don't forget Tablet PC support (along with ClearType enhancements, which make text easier to read on LCD displays)—a big coup for brainstormers, doodlers, and those who spend much of their days away from their desks, sitting around conference tables.

Outlook extends online messaging capability to make it easy for you to see who's online and contact them instantly with a quick question or meeting request. Great improvements in both the look and feel and the function of Outlook make organizing and working with messages and appointments easier and more intuitive. A new Reading Pane gives you considerably more room onscreen to view selected messages, and smart folders and new views give you options for storing and working with information.

> **Tip**   Outlook's junk e-mail filtering has been greatly improved in Office 2003. A new filtering system evaluates the structure of individual messages to determine whether they should be classified as "junk;" this is a major change from the sender-based blocking system used in Office XP. Additionally, lists for trusted senders and trusted receivers help users control their incoming and outgoing mail. For more about new junk e-mail filtering features in Outlook, see Chapter 2, "Microsoft Office Outlook 2003 and Messaging."

Excel's big news is support for XML and the increased functionality of smart tags. Excel also links up nicely to the improved list functionality in SharePoint Team Services, which enables you to publish specific ranges from a worksheet to a SharePoint list for review or discussion. Lists on a SharePoint Team Services site can be exported to Excel for easy reporting and list-maintenance tasks. The Tablet PC is now supported in Excel as well, so you can add notes to a document, edit a worksheet by hand, or circle key workbook elements that you feel need expansion.

PowerPoint has dropped the Pack and Go Wizard and replaced it with a Package to CD option, which enables you to create PowerPoint presentations that anyone can view, with or without PowerPoint. For the first time, smart tags also are available in PowerPoint, a major help for business presenters and developers who want to give viewers options for more information. Another big change is PowerPoint's integration with Microsoft Windows Media Player; now you can run video and include streaming audio in your presentations on the fly.

Access now supports XML and smart tags, enabling developers to create new, feature-rich help sets for end users and managers. Like Excel, Access now links to SharePoint Team Services, allowing you to share table data with others on your team or download information into an Access table for analyzing or reporting. Other functionality improvements include better error-checking for forms and reports, context-sensitive help when you're building SQL queries, and a new backup database option in the File menu that lets you create a backup while you work.

FrontPage takes a major step in this release toward working more comfortably with the variety of Web browsers, environments, and development languages that are currently in use on the Web. You can easily work in numerous browsers now and code in HTML if you choose without wading through the stock code earlier versions of FrontPage placed for you. It's cleaner, faster, and more flexible.

From the Experts

Jim Buyens, author of *Microsoft Office FrontPage 2003 Inside Out*, expects that the addition of dynamic templates, layout tables, and the new, elaborate editor in FrontPage 2003 will be a hit with developers. The lists, subwebs, and Web Parts in SharePoint Team Services also create interesting possibilities for development possibilities. When asked whether he would recommend that current FrontPage users upgrade to FrontPage 2003, he replied: "Absolutely. It's worth the upgrade just for the coding features alone."

Other productivity enhancements include changes in Microsoft Office Document Imaging, which includes smarter OCR (optical character recognition) software that enables you to convert scanned images into text, illustrations, and tables for export into Word. The improvements in Office Document Imaging can also help you with those non-Office documents you don't know what to do with; you can receive them as digital images and then convert them into the form you need that works with your other Office applications.

Finally, the new Microsoft Picture Library gives you an image toolkit for making simple edits to your digital images. You can compress, crop, edit, rotate, and change the brightness and contrast of pictures by using the editing features in the Picture Library. You can also use the Picture Library to rename the images you download from your digital camera, and you can share photos and diagrams with others using SharePoint Team Services.

> **More Info**   You'll learn more about the various improvements and additions in each of the core Office applications in Chapter 8, "Microsoft Office 2003 Productivity Enhancements."

Summary

As you can see, Office 2003 includes great changes that make communicating faster, collaborating easier, sharing data smarter, and tailoring applications to your specific business needs more intuitive than ever. With new features for the end user and developer, this new Office—which represents a huge step in the direction of integrating and streamlining business processes—is *definitely* worth a closer look.

2

Microsoft Office Outlook 2003 and Messaging

Much of what we communicate is information about information. We write messages, memos, and reports and create spreadsheets, presentations, and Web pages to show others—down the hall or around the world—what we want them to know about our businesses, products, plans, and people. But evolving technology in the increasingly connected world has brought about changes that continue to streamline and expedite the way we view and use information—and the way we communicate—in our jobs and lives.

Today communication is information; the notes we jot down, the words we speak, the sketches we draw, and the circles and boxes on a presentation whiteboard all contribute important data bits to the larger whole. The ability to capture and save that information in a usable form, and share it instantly with coworkers or team members, ensures that our best ideas can be preserved and applied as quickly as possible, which can make a difference in the way we do business over the long term. Innovation, the sharing of ideas, and the smart use of technology—all are good things.

This chapter explores the additions and enhancements in Microsoft Outlook 2003—and there's a lot of ground to cover. Because communication and collaboration is one of the focal points of the far-reaching changes in Microsoft Office 2003, Outlook is the application sporting the most noticeable modifications. Let's begin where it's most apparent: in the user interface.

A New Look for Outlook

New colors and a fresh design pick up on the look and feel of Microsoft Windows XP and its theme-related motif in Office 2003. You'll find a number of improvements in the interface that make better use of available screen space and more efficient use of your time. One thing you'll notice is that the Favorites menu (did anyone really use that in Outlook anyway?) has been traded for the Go menu, which offers options and shortcut keys for moving among the various Outlook views (plus Journal).

Icons are helpful, but not at the expense of on-screen workspace. That's one of the clear messages of Outlook's new look. The icon bar that stretched down the left side of Outlook XP has been replaced with a more functional Navigation Pane, which includes the Folder List in the default view. (See Figure 2-1.)

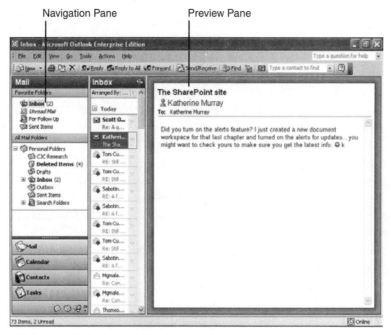

Figure 2-1 The new look of Microsoft Outlook gives you more viewing room on-screen and makes better use of available space.

By default, the four primary Outlook view bars (Mail, Calendar, Contacts, and Tasks) occupy a space in the lower third of the Navigation Pane. The views that don't appear by default (Notes, Folder List, and Shortcuts) are available as icons at the bottom of the pane. You can expand the view bars to show all the selections by dragging the separator bar upward; or you can collapse the list to show the various views only as icons along the bottom of the Navigation Pane. This gives you more room for displaying and selecting the mail folders you need to use.

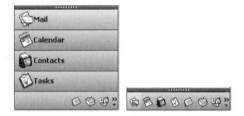

The new three-column layout in Outlook condenses quite a bit of information into one viewing space, but it also provides more room for the new-and-improved Preview Pane, making it easy for you to scan a message quickly without scrolling, which saves both time and trouble. The claim is that the revised Preview Pane now gives you 40 percent more area for e-mail viewing, but whatever the percentage (which changes depending on how wide you make the Inbox column), it makes mail easier to move through quickly—which is something most of us need.

Tip   Another perk of the Preview Pane: for users who work with Outlook on backlit LCD screens (for example, on Pocket and Tablet PCs), ClearType technology and changes in spacing and character positioning will make reading text—even on the smallest screens—easier.

Working with Views

The increased viewing area in the Outlook window is helpful no matter which view you use. The new layout makes better use of available space but also offers you many options for viewing your information the way you want to see it. Each of the Outlook views has several key improvements or enhancements to help you organize and display your data in the way that makes most sense to you.

Mail Improvements

Mail view is displayed by default when you first start Outlook, with the Inbox in the center column, the selected message displayed in the improved Preview Pane, and the folders in the Navigation Pane on the far left side of the window. The design makes it easy for you to see what a message is about quickly and then decide whether to discard it, leave it in the Inbox, or drag it to the Follow Up folder for later action. This helps you handle the volume of e-mail—both wanted and unwanted—that flows across your desktop all day long.

The major change in Mail view is increased area for the Preview Pane (in most cases, allowing you to read most of an average-length e-mail message without scrolling) and the new Navigation Pane, which houses the folders you'll use to organize and act on important messages.

You can arrange messages in a variety of different ways (this is an enhancement of the Current View feature available previously). To change the way messages are displayed, choose Arrange By from the View menu and select one of the many fields by which you want to sort and display messages. Figure 2-2 shows the menu choices available to you. (Note that you can still use the Current View selections if you choose.)

Figure 2-2   You can arrange your e-mail to best suit the type of work you do.

Suppose, for example, that you are compiling a report that includes sections written by each of your company's five major departments. The deadline is fast approaching, and you've sent each of the department managers notes asking them to submit their reports by the end of the day. You can use Arrange By to set your Mail view to Attachments so that Outlook separates the messages with attachments from those without. The messages with attachments are displayed at the top of the Inbox, where you'll see them first; other messages are organized in the No Attachments section below. This lets you check at a glance and make sure all the reports are in by day's end as you prepare for a long night of compiling and editing the final document.

More Info   Of course, you could use SharePoint Team Services and the new shared Document Workspace feature to assign, track, and work with document pieces and versions. For more about SharePoint Team Services, see Chapter 3.

Calendar Changes

In Calendar view, the Work Week view is shown by default in the Reading Pane, and a monthly calendar and links to your personal and shared calendars are displayed in the Navigation Pane. (See Figure 2-3.) You can create new appointments, set up meetings, look at shared calendars, change the look of the calendar, and create and view team schedules by clicking the familiar tools on the toolbar.

Figure 2-3 Calendar view provides more room for the selected calendar display, along with a monthly view and links to other calendars on the left.

> **Note** You can display the TaskPad in the rightmost column of Calendar by choosing TaskPad from the View menu. Another new feature in Office 2003: you can customize the tasks displayed in the TaskPad by selecting the TaskPad View option in the View menu when Calendar view is active.

Enhancements in Contacts View

In Contacts view, the Preview Pane displays contacts in alphabetical order, but you can easily modify the display of contacts by clicking one of the view options in the Navigation Pane:

- Address Cards (the default) displays the contact name and e-mail address.

- Detailed Address Cards shows all available information on the General tab of the person's contact file.

- Phone List displays contact names and phone numbers only.

- By Category shows the contacts organized by assigned categories.

> **Tip**   Outlook includes a master list of categories that you can use as is or modify to suit your business or personal needs. To add a category designation quickly to individual contacts without opening the Contact window, right-click a contact and choose Categories from the context menu; click the category you want, and then click OK.

- By Company lists contacts alphabetically by company name.

- Location uses the Country/By Region field (displayed in the Check Addresses window) to sort and display contacts according to country and region.

- By Follow-Up Flag shows all flagged contacts first in the displayed list.

Being able to change how contacts are displayed makes it easier for you to create a subset of contacts for a specific project. Suppose you've identified six key people to participate in an upcoming diversity program offered by the HR department. You can go through your contacts and flag potential representatives from each major department; then in Contacts view, use By Follow-Up Flag to list those contacts together at the top of the contacts list. You can then right-click to display the context menu and choose Forward Items. This attaches the contact info for the employees to an e-mail message that you can then send to the head of HR. All this will take just a few minutes (or less, depending on the number of contacts you had to consider), and you can mark another item off your Tasks list.

Improvements in Tasks View and TaskPad

Speaking of Tasks, the Tasks view now has additional display controls as well. You can display tasks using one of these views: Simple List, Detailed List, Active Tasks, Next Seven Days, Overdue Tasks, By Category, Assignment, By Person Responsible, Completed Tasks, or Task Timeline. Additionally, you can open Shared Tasks and customize the current task view by choosing the options at the bottom of the Navigation Pane. If you want to change the way tasks appear in the TaskPad (shown in the left column in Calendar view), you can choose TaskPad View from the View menu and select from the available options:

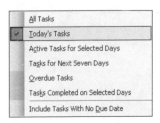

A New Look for the Address Book

In addition to the new look in the various Outlook views, a change has also been made to an often-used dialog box. In response to customer requests, the Select Names dialog box in the Windows Address Book has been revamped. Now when users click To: to select the recipient for an e-mail message, they can drag the borders of the dialog box to resize it and display more information about their contacts.

(continued)

A New Look for the Address Book   *(continued)*

The recipient buttons (To, Cc, and Bcc) are now placed below the display area, making the process more intuitive for users who want to select multiple contacts, and then add the selected contacts to the appropriate recipient line.

One note, however: If you're wondering where to find the New Contact button, click Advanced to display a menu of the familiar contact management commands.

Streamlining E-Mail

If you're like most of us, the sheer volume of the e-mail you receive in a day has increased dramatically. Not only do we sift through spam in various forms, but more and more people are using e-mail as the communication channel of choice. There's logic behind that—e-mail is fast, simple, and you can read and respond when it's convenient for you, which is a great consideration if you attend meeting after meeting throughout the day and rarely find the time during business hours to return phone calls, for example.

E-mail is fast, convenient, and flexible, but it can get out of control quickly. When you receive interdepartmental e-mail and e-mail from service vendors and suppliers, prospective customers and long-term clients, your boss and your boss's boss, various industry publications, and friends and family, the volume can become unmanageable fast.

Realizing that people who work with information need a way to sort it quickly (which messages do you need to read right away, and which ones can you read later?) and a simple way to organize and store what's important, the developers of Outlook added several features that enable you to see the messages coming in and act on them accordingly.

One time-saving feature is the prompt that appears as a message is downloading. When a new message arrives, a message alert pops up in the lower right corner of the Outlook window showing the sender's name, the subject, and the first few words of the incoming message. You can skim the information in the message and opt whether to stop what you're doing and read the entire message or simply let it go to the Inbox where you can read it later.

Another small-but-helpful time-saving feature: a message info tag appears when you position the cursor over a selected message, giving you information about the sender, the date and time the message was sent, and the subject and size of the message. This can be helpful when you're looking for a particular message but don't want to expand the Inbox column or read through too many subject lines.

```
From: Katherine Murray
Received: Wed 1/29/2003
12:31 PM
Subject: RE: A question :)
Size: 17 KB
```

If you often find yourself scrolling through dozens of old messages, looking for the specific one you want, you'll love the Arrange by Conversation option that allows you to display messages as threaded conversations. This option groups all messages with a related subject together so that you can easily find the one you're looking for. The new messages are displayed at the top of the thread, and unread messages are nested beneath. Click on the expand button to see past messages related to that subject, and click the collapse button to hide the display of the messages when you no longer need them. (See Figure 2-4.)

Figure 2-4   The new Arrange by Conversation thread lets you organize your messages by the topic of discussion, so you can easily see all messages related to a certain online conversation.

A New Emphasis on Collaboration

Communication and collaboration are two keystones in the entire Office 2003 release. Collaborating on projects—whether you're producing an annual report, hosting a conference, putting together a presentation, designing a corporate Web site, or developing a new product prototype—means that everyone involved needs access to critical information, a way to get together to plan strategy and discuss problems, and a method of making specific task assignments so that each member of the team knows what to do.

This version of Outlook gives collaboration an entirely new focus. Although past releases had support for group scheduling and online meetings, Outlook 2003 includes the tools, functionality, and templates team leaders can use so that their teams can communicate instantly, share ideas easily, and organize and manage projects using simple, list-oriented Web-based tools.

Instant Messaging and Notifications

Instant messaging with Windows Messenger is spread far and wide throughout Office 2003. Whenever you use a Contact name—in a Microsoft Office Word document, an Excel spreadsheet, a PowerPoint slide, or in an Outlook message header—a smart tag gives you the ability to contact that person directly from the document you're working in. For example, suppose that you're in the middle of setting up a product review meeting for this afternoon. It's short notice, and you're not sure whether you should schedule it for today or tomorrow. You open Calendar and take a look at the group schedule; when you position the pointer over the team leader's name, an instant messaging icon appears, telling you that the team leader is online. You can click the icon to display the context menu and then send an instant message, asking whether to meet today or tomorrow.

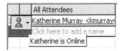

Instant messaging works seamlessly in Outlook. When you're using other applications, it works like this: If you have smart tags enabled on your system (in Word, Excel, and PowerPoint go to the Tools menu and choose AutoCorrect Options; then choose the Smart Tags tab, and select Label text with smart tags), the name of any person in your Contacts list appears with a dotted purple underline. When you position the pointer on the underline, a small Smart Tag Actions button appears. Click it to see whether the person is currently online, and you'll also see a list of communications choices for sending a message to the person named.

Similarly, when you are working in Outlook and you receive a message, the header of the message shows whether the sender is one of your online contacts. If the sender is currently online (and has either a Hotmail account or a .NET Passport), the instant message icon appears in color and the smart tag displays an action menu that enables you to reply with an instant message or an e-mail message, open the person's Contact information, schedule a meeting, and more. (See Figure 2-5.)

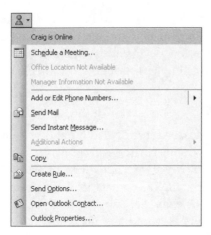

Figure 2-5   When you receive e-mail from an online contact, an instant message icon in the header lets you know whether the sender is currently online.

Having immediate access to online team members carries over into the other applications as well. When you're working in Word, Excel, or PowerPoint, whenever the name of one of your online contacts appears in a document (or in the document workspace or Shared Workspace task pane), the same "pawn" indicator will let you know whether the person is currently online. Click to display the context menu and send a message or modify the person's contact options.

This seamless integration of messaging and applications lets you send off a quick question—"What is the official title of that report?"—or ask for clarification—"Did you want me to use the Verdana or Arial font for the article content?" as you're working on your projects. This saves time and effort and reduces the likelihood that an important question will be forgotten and a critical detail overlooked.

> **Note**   Instant messaging and online presence information is also available on SharePoint Team Services sites, allowing you to see when other team members are online and send them an instant message on the spot.

Comparing Schedules

One of the challenges to successful collaboration is getting everyone on the same page—and in the same space—at the same time. Setting up meetings everyone can attend is tricky when you need to coordinate half a dozen busy professionals. The new side-by-side calendaring feature in Outlook gives you the ability to share your calendar with others and view others' calendars by placing them beside your own. That way, you can easily see which time slots are open for everyone and which are definitely a no go.

> **Note**   You can open others' calendars only if you are using Microsoft Exchange.

You begin side-by-side calendaring by sharing your own calendar. In the Navigation Pane of the Calendar window, click the Share My Calendar link. Then enter the information of the person (or people) with permission to view your Calendar, and click OK. This enables others to view your information.

To view others' calendars next to yours, click Open A Shared Calendar and type the person's name, or choose it from your Contacts list. The other person must have previously selected Share My Calendar in his or her version of Outlook and given you permission to view the calendar before you will be allowed access. The other person's calendar is added to your Other Calendars list. To display calendars in side-by-side format, simply click the checkboxes of the calendars you want to see.

Side-by-side calendar view displayed each person's daily calendar in a separate column, enabling you to see at a glance when others are available. (See Figure 2-6.)

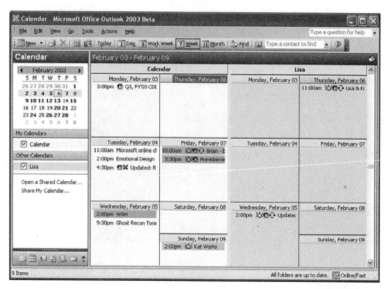

Figure 2-6   The side-by-side calendar view displays multiple calendars in a columnar format.

Free/Busy the Internet Way

If you want to share information with people who don't have access to your Calendar, you can use the Microsoft Office Internet Free/Busy Service, a free service that enables you to share your calendar information and see the schedules of others who sign up. For more information, go to the Web site: *freebusy.office.microsoft.com/freebusy.*

You can also set up the Free/Busy service from within Outlook by opening the Tools menu and choosing Options, clicking the Calendar Options button, and clicking the Free/Busy Options button. In the Free/Busy Options dialog box, click Manage. You are taken to the Free/Busy site, where you can set up the service and add the users to whom you want to give access to your schedule.

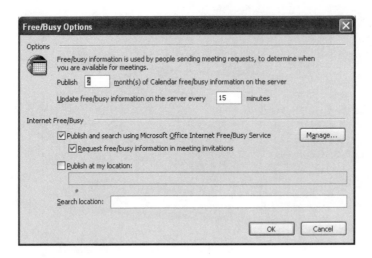

Meeting Workspaces

Getting people together in the same time and space is important, so Outlook also provides the means for workgroups to gather in a meeting workspace on the Web. If your company uses SharePoint Team Services V2 (STS) or SharePoint Portal Services (SPS), you can create shared workspaces with documents, photos, presentations, discussions, and more, all related to an upcoming meeting or critical event.

You create a meeting workspace by clicking the Meeting Workspace button in the Appointment window. The Meeting Workspace task pane opens so that you can create a new workspace or select an existing one. (See Figure 2-7.)

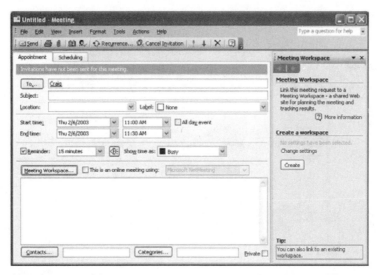

Figure 2-7   In the Meeting Workspace task pane, you can create or edit workspaces.

If your company uses SharePoint Team Services, you can create a shared meeting space on the Web where team members can meet and share information. The actual Meeting Workspace is a subweb—a Web site within a SharePoint Team Services site—that allows you to gather important information and prepare for an upcoming meeting. For example, suppose that you have put together a team to prepare for your company's next annual meeting. You have two months to plan, documents and presentations to prepare, an auditorium to reserve, multimedia equipment to secure, and awards to procure.

Meeting Workspaces offer a number of different templates that will enable you to set up the workspace you need for a particular meeting. Figure 2-8, on the next page, shows an example of a Meeting Workspace. For more about creating and working with Meeting Workspaces, see Chapter 3, "Collaborating Using SharePoint Team Services and SharePoint Portal Server."

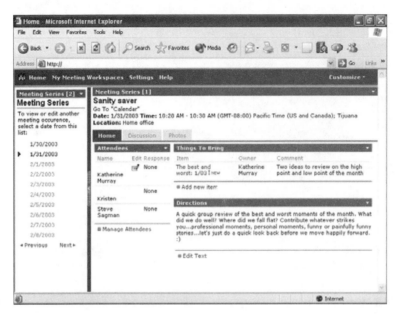

Figure 2-8   An example of a Meeting Workspace created using SharePoint Team Services V2.

More Effective E-Mail Management

A number of the features in Outlook are meant simply to make you more productive while working with the program. Think of the time you lose in searching for, selecting, and organizing specific messages related to a particular product, person, or event. Outlook 2003 includes several features to help you manage your e-mail more effectively and efficiently. This section introduces you to search folders, fast RSVPs to meeting invitations, the quick flag capability, as well as the improved rules interface and the brand-new alerts feature, which ties you in to updates on your SharePoint Team Services sites.

> **Tip**   Let's mention a quick functionality feature first. Thanks to user responses, the Office team has improved the AutoComplete feature that adds recognized names in the recipient lines of your e-mail messages. Now Outlook matches names as soon as you type one letter and displays your most-often-used contact names first.

Using Search Folders

At first glance, you might think that search folders actually store the results of a search for messages about specific projects, people, or things. In reality, search folders are like filtered views, showing you only the information you want to see without actually removing the messages from their place in the Inbox.

Outlook 2003 comes with several search folders already created: For Follow Up will display any e-mail messages you flag; Large Messages will display messages arranged from largest to smallest; Unread Messages will show you all the unread messages you've accumulated. You can create your own search folders by right-clicking an existing search folder and choosing New Search Folder from the context menu. In the New Search Folder dialog box, you can choose one of the existing templates or create a custom folder based on criteria you specify. (See Figure 2-9.)

> **Tip**   You can use other commands in the Search Folder context menu to customize the display of search folders and move them up or down in the displayed list.

Figure 2-9   You can use one of the predefined templates to create a search folder or start from scratch.

You might use Search Folders in your organization to store messages from your favorite clients, track the results from a recent online promotion, collect information about personal vacation days, gather all correspondence related to a specific product, or store copies of all departmental e-newsletters.

Quick Handling of Invitations

In Outlook 2003, you can quickly accept or decline (or mark as tentative) a meeting invitation you receive without even opening the e-mail message. When a meeting invitation arrives in your Inbox, you'll see immediately the response line stretched across the top of the message (you don't even need to open the message to see it).

You can simply click your choice in the top of the message while it is displayed in the Preview Pane and a response is automatically sent to the sender. If you prefer, you can respond by right-clicking the message to display the context-sensitive menu and choose the option that fits your choice (Accept, Tentative, Decline, Propose New Time, or Check Calendar).

Quick Flag Capability

Remember the Flag for Follow-Up capability in Office XP? It has grown exponentially in Office 2003. Now the Quick Flag feature enables you to mark a variety of items in your Inbox for follow-up and organize them by up to six different colors.

> **Note**   You might want to create an Outlook note to generate a flag legend to remind yourself of the meaning of each color.

After you've finished flagging items, you can view them as a group by clicking the For Follow Up folder in the Navigation Pane. Outlook displays all the flagged items, arranged according to their color type. (See Figure 2-10.)

Figure 2-10   Displaying flagged items in the For Follow Up search folder shows that they are divided by color.

When you complete the follow-up on one of the flagged items, simply click the flag to remove it.

Easy Editing of Distribution Lists

If you regularly publish e-mail newsletters, department updates, or product listings that you distribute to a number of people, you probably are already using distribution lists to help you expedite the process. (A distribution list is group of e-mail contacts that you group and name. You can send a message to everyone on the list by entering only the distribution list name in the To: line of an e-mail message.)

Now, in Outlook 2003, you can easily add to or remove names from the distribution list before sending a message. This would enable you to send out the new spring product listing to everyone on the distribution list except the two people who received their copies in a face-to-face meeting. To modify the distribution list for this one use, you simply enter the list name in the To: line as usual; then click the expand button to the left of the list name to expand the list.

To...	⊞ **Office News**
Cc...	
Subject:	

You can then edit the names as needed by removing or adding additional contacts. When you're ready, click Send and the message is distributed as usual.

For those International Messages

Now Outlook 2003 offers unlimited support for the Multilingual User Interface, which means that network administrators can choose the interface and help files needed for specific languages. Unicode is now supported for Mail, Calendar, Contacts, Tasks, and Note, which enables users to see and work with text in any language recognized by the operating system.

Working with E-Mail Rules and Alerts

You can streamline the time you spend reading through message after message by automating the process with rules. Rules are actions Outlook performs based on specific criteria you set for handling specific types of messages. For example, you might want to forward to your customer service manager all the messages received from the marketing department; or you might send all messages from a certain vendor to the person in charge of managing that relationship.

Rules existed as the Rules Wizard in earlier versions of Office; in Office 2003, the Rules interface has been enhanced, new templates have been added, and an entirely new feature—alerts—has been included. Figure 2-11 shows the new look for the Rules Wizard.

Figure 2-11 The Rules Wizard is easier to follow and includes additional templates.

You don't have to use the Rules Wizard to create rules for organizing and storing your e-mail messages, however. The process can be as simple as this: When you receive an e-mail message you want to create a rule for, right-click the header of the message. In the context menu, choose Create Rule. You can then easily specify the settings for the rule, and click OK to create it. You might, for example, opt to have all messages from a particular company placed in a certain folder; or you might want to play a sound for messages with high importance.

If you're running SharePoint Team Services V2, you can receive e-mail alerts whenever a document is updated, reviewed, modified, or commented on or an announcement is added to your SharePoint Team Services site. This enables you to keep up to date with the latest happenings online with your project or workgroup. You can select a similar set of actions for alerts you create on the site. (See Figure 2-12.)

Figure 2-12   You can assign similar actions to the alert notification coming in from your SharePoint Team Services site.

More Info   For more about setting up and working with alerts in SharePoint Team Services, see Chapter 3.

Security and Privacy

To make sending and receiving information more secure for Office 2003 users, Outlook continues enhanced support for certificates and now shares the authentication list stored by Internet Explorer that tracks approved sites. You can also customize signatures for each e-mail on your account, which allows you to have one professional signature for your work e-mail and another signature for family and friends.

To better protect your privacy and take a first major offensive step against spam, this version of Outlook 2003 enables you to block HTML content and keep junk mail senders from gathering information from your computer. When you receive a piece of junk mail with HTML that refers to external content (such as a rotating image or logo), you'll notice that there is a short wait while the image appears. During this time, the e-mail message notifies the sender that it "found" your address and sends back to get the information to fill in the graphic. This data transfer capability is known as a web beacon, and it simply lets the junk mail provider know that your e-mail address is live. As a result, you can be sure you'll continue to receive plenty of spam from this vendor and hundreds more like it.

When Outlook blocks external HTML content, the program keeps the data transfer from happening because the message doesn't go back to the external source to display the logo file. This keeps the site from knowing whether your address is "live," which eventually lessens the amount of junk mail you receive. Figure 2-13 shows an example of an e-mail message sent with blocked information in the header.

Figure 2-13 Outlook blocks external HTML in an attempt to limit the spam you receive.

Enhanced Junk E-mail Filters

Outlook 2003 uses a new junk e-mail filtering system to evaluate and weed out the unwanted messages in your Inbox. The filter looks at the content and structure of a message to determine whether it is likely to be junk; if it's determined to be junk, the mail is deposited in a Junk E-mail folder, where you can review and delete it later. Additional features that help you regain control of your Inbox include these:

- To ensure that mail from welcome senders isn't treated as junk e-mail, you can add known senders to a Trusted Senders List. By default, all the contacts in your Outlook Contacts are automatically included on this list.

- To block e-mail from a certain sender, you can add the sender to the Junk Senders List. This blocks all future messages from the specified sender.

- If you want to ensure that e-mail you send to certain recipients will not be blocked as junk e-mail, you can create a Trusted Recipients List.

- You can get periodic updates for the junk e-mail filter by downloading them from microsoft.com.

From the Experts

Michael Young, author of *Microsoft Office 2003 Professional Edition Inside Out*, had this to say about the new external content blocking and filtering in Outlook: "The thing that really jazzes me is this simple little thing in Outlook where it blocks content when you open an HTML message. It's a nice little feature—one that touches on the way I work." Michael, who is also the author of *XML Step by Step*, sees great potential for developers in the widespread support for XML in this release. "XML is the new area for solutions development," he says, noting that the extensive support for industry-standard XML and the ability to work with any kind of arbitrary schema in Office 2003 will present solutions to developers with a huge range of development opportunities.

Additional Input Options

How many ways can you create an e-mail message? Now in Office 2003, you can dictate a message or write one by hand. With Tablet PC support throughout Office 2003, which is even further enhanced by the addition of the exciting, new OneNote utility, you can handwrite notes or use the stylus or keyboard to input message text to your Tablet PC and then send as normal. You can use a microphone and the Speech option (available in the Tools menu) to begin the process.

> **More Info**   To find out more about OneNote, the new utility in Office 2003 that enables you to track, record, write, store, organize, and use notes, recordings, doodles, and diagrams, see Chapter 4, "Introduction to Microsoft Office OneNote 2003."

Changes in the E-Mail Message Window

While we're talking about functionality, there are a few new tools in the Outlook toolbar worth mentioning. The Options button has been moved to a more prominent position on the toolbar, saving you the trouble of digging through menus to set options for individual messages.

You also now have the ability to choose on the fly the format for the e-mail message you want to send. Selection choices are HTML, Rich Text, or Plain Text. This will be helpful when you send to clients whose e-mail services are different from your own.

In addition, while you're creating a message, you can click Flag in the Outlook toolbar to display the Flag for Follow-Up dialog box and set an action and the date and time you want the follow-up to be completed. You also can digitally sign or encrypt individual messages by clicking the Digitally Sign button on the Message toolbar. (See Figure 2-14.)

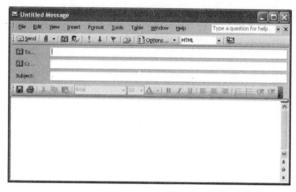

Figure 2-14   Office 2003 includes a number of new tools in the message toolbar that enable you to customize the actions, format, and signature of individual messages.

One more key feature you'll recognize: The new Table menu in the menu bar borrows all its key options from an existing Office application. If you're familiar with tables in Word, you'll be comfortable using these features in your e-mail messages as well.

Summary

This chapter has highlighted the key changes in Outlook 2003. Specifically, you've learned about the changes in the layout of the Outlook window and how you can tailor many of the views to display data so that it best fits your process. You've also found out more about the expanded collaboration features in Outlook and learned about side-by-side calendars and shared Meeting Workspaces. Finally, this chapter detailed a number of Outlook features that help increase your productivity, shorten your e-mail–processing time, and protect your privacy. The next chapter takes a closer look at SharePoint Team Services and the expanded collaboration features built into Office 2003.

3

Collaborating Using SharePoint Team Services and SharePoint Portal Server

Microsoft SharePoint technology—a group of products and services that make organizing, sharing, and finding information a seamless part of an information worker's daily tasks—is at the heart of the collaborative nature of Microsoft Office 2003. With features built into each of the core Office applications, users can collaborate on documents, check group schedules, send instant messages, organize meetings, transfer data to and from applications using the familiar Office environment, and move easily from their desktops to their SharePoint Team Services (STS) group sites and back again.

This chapter gives you a first look at SharePoint Team Services version 2 and SharePoint technology and describes the specific collaboration and communication enhancements in SharePoint Team Services that make it easier than ever to work collaboratively in a corporate—or global—environment.

The SharePoint Technologies Vision

The vision for SharePoint Team Services and SharePoint Portal Server is a tightly integrated set of products that enable users in groups of all sizes to access, share, find, store, update, work with, and manage information. Are you creating a training curriculum for your IT department? You can use SharePoint Team Services to manage the project, hold meetings, discuss changes, make revisions, and approve, publish, and distribute the final materials. Do you need a full-spectrum information-management system that gives employees access to resources both inside and outside your company intranet? SharePoint Portal Team Services includes Team Services and adds powerful search features and enhanced document-management capabilities so that you can customize and extend the reach of the sites and systems you create.

A First Look at SharePoint Team Services

SharePoint Team Services was first available to millions of users as a Microsoft FrontPage 2002 template that enabled users to create collaborative team Web sites for small workgroups. The technology offered a list-based service and an easy-to-use, customizable interface, giving informal teams a way to organize and share information on intranets and the Web at large. In Office 2003, Share-Point Team Services (now built on Microsoft Windows .NET Server technology) has been significantly enhanced and integrated with each of the core applications, adding new collaboration features and providing ways for you to keep current with your projects and groups.

Although SharePoint is a relatively new offering, it has a short learning curve: the site is simple to use and understand, and users can move easily among their Office applications to the SharePoint site and back again. In fact, depending on your specific task, you might use SharePoint Team Services without actually appearing to "move to" the SharePoint Team Services site. Microsoft Office Word 2003 offers one example of this: when you click the Tools menu in Word and choose Shared Workspace, the Shared Workspace task pane opens along the right side of the Word window. (See Figure 3-1.)

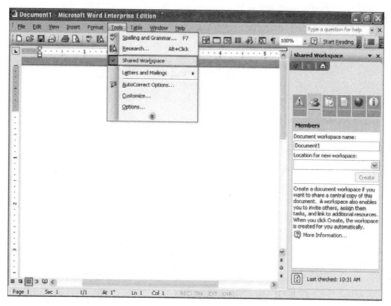

Figure 3-1   Access to SharePoint Team Services is built into each of the core Office applications.

Information in the Shared Workspace task pane related to your current document is actually part of SharePoint Team Services, but you don't have to access the site to see it; it's brought to you. The Shared Workspace pane first gives you the option of creating a document workspace for your current document; later the workspace displays the names and online status of others collaborating on that document, any tasks that have been assigned for it, and links to related documents and resource information. This brings you the information you need and gives you access to instant communication and resources with a click of the mouse—without your ever leaving the current document.

SharePoint Team Services also gives users a central point of access and data sharing by creating a Web site accessible from within the various Office applications. You have many different entrance points—in Microsoft Office Outlook 2003, you can create a Meeting Workspace, which takes you to the SharePoint Team Services site. (See Figure 3-2, on the next page.) In Microsoft Office FrontPage 2003, you can create and modify the STS sites for your group. In Microsoft Office Excel 2003 and Access 2003, you can import and export data from the various lists you organize and manage on your SharePoint site.

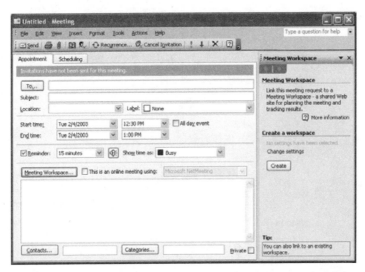

Figure 3-2 You can create a new meeting workspace in Outlook when you send out your regular meeting requests.

The SharePoint Team Services site is built on a list-based concept, enabling you to create lists of announcements, events, links, and more. (See Figure 3-3.) The sites are easy to customize and contribute to; team members can easily share thoughts, documents, pictures, calendars, and more. Instant-messaging capability lets users see at a glance who is online, so they can send a quick question if they choose; and the Web discussions feature enables members to review and share their thoughts without altering the files or sites being discussed.

Tip The "pawn" indicator beside an author name shows that this person is currently online. You can display a context menu of communication choices by positioning the pointer over the indicator and clicking the down arrow that appears.

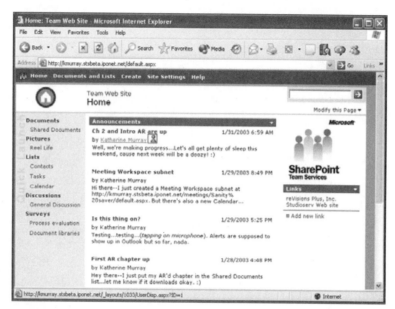

Figure 3-3   The SharePoint Team Services Web sites are list-based, offering users a variety of simple ways to add, modify, view, and organize information.

What Can You Do with SharePoint Team Services?

SharePoint Team Services in Office 2003 is built on Windows .NET Server and SQL Server, which among other things enables it to take advantage of the full standards-based XML support built into the infrastructure of Office 2003. This means that you can upload and download lists seamlessly to and from SharePoint Team Services sites, outputting them as XML data that can be used in many different ways. This is just one small part of what SharePoint Team Services offers in this release. The following list gives you a fuller picture of what you can do with SharePoint Team Services, whether you're an end user creating a simple group site or a developer extending the functionality of existing services:

■   Work collaboratively—sharing documents, assigning tasks, and managing processes—with other members of a team or workgroup.

- Contribute to your team Web site from anywhere you have Web access.

- Communicate instantly with other team members who are currently online.

- Use lists to post, update, store, and download information from the team site.

- View information the way you want it using SharePoint's flexible views and filtering capabilities.

- View information from SharePoint in Outlook and access shared contacts and side-by-side calendars for easier scheduling.

- Create and work on shared documents in a live workspace as part of SharePoint Team Services.

- Store team documents in document libraries so that they can be shared, updated, approved, and distributed by assigned team members.

- Give individual team members site permissions according to their role on the team; prevent sensitive data from being displayed in searches conducted without necessary permissions.

- Use alerts to receive notification whenever updates occur on the SharePoint Team Services site.

- Customize your team site by modifying individual Web Parts.

- Create online surveys for team members.

- Hold Web discussions online in discussion threads that are stored independently (no need for tracking or checking documents in and out).

Who Uses SharePoint Team Services?

SharePoint Team Services gives employees in small- to medium-size teams features that can help them work easily together on shared projects. The group could comprise employees from one department of a larger company, employees from various departments, or workers scattered across the country or the globe. SharePoint Team Services runs on Windows .NET Server 2003, but team members contributing to the site can add, upload, comment on, and work with documents and lists, and communicate with team members from any point of Web access.

Specifically, these groups (and many more) could use SharePoint Team Services:

- A workgroup organizing an annual meeting for an insurance company

- An HR team charged with evaluating, discussing, selecting, and administering a new benefits package

- A software development group testing and discussing its newest product

- A group of trainers organizing a shared conference from separate locations

- A publishing team collaborating on a fast-track book

- A recruiting firm creating a proposal for outplacement services on behalf of a major corporation

- An IT work team organizing system training materials for new hires

- A small accounting firm preparing a tax summary package for preferred clients

- A financial planning and analysis group that needs to stay in touch with ongoing training, new materials, industry news, and more

- A legal team collecting data; organizing resources; and writing, revising, and discussing a developing project

When users need a Web site they can create and contribute to immediately, SharePoint Team Services is ready with an out-of-the-box answer. The easy-to-use interface, integration with familiar Office applications, and simple list-management features make it easy for collaborating information workers to create, organize, and manage data and documents in a way that works best for them.

A First Look at SharePoint Portal Server

While SharePoint Team Services is the answer to individual workgroups focusing on individual projects and events, SharePoint Portal Server sits on top of Team Services, adding the extended functionality of an enterprise portal. SharePoint Portal Server can be used in a single work area (similar to SharePoint Team Services), but its real power extends company-wide, providing those with the necessary permissions (employees, vendors, clients, and others) access to powerful search features; indexing capabilities; sophisticated document-management tools and processes; and a customizable, modular Web-publishing system that enables departments to publish and provide subscription features to deliver relevant content to users in various areas. Because SharePoint Portal Server works seamlessly with the most familiar Office applications and a Web browser, users are working in an environment they already know.

Overview of New Features in SharePoint 2

Whether you use SharePoint Portal Server or SharePoint Team Services, the new collaboration, communication, and functionality features integrated with the Office 2003 applications enable you to share data and documents easily; organize your information, announcements, and lists in a common space; interact with team members on the fly; and use the data you gather in your daily Office tasks. This section gives you a closer look at the new SharePoint Team Services features included with Office 2003.

New Collaborative Productivity Solutions

An old rule of thumb goes something like this: Getting something done by committee takes about four times as long as doing it yourself. There tends to be a lot of hurry-up-and-wait when you're working in groups. There's the challenge of getting everybody in the same place at the same time; splitting the workload up into tasks that can be accomplished by each member; making sure everyone on the team has the resources to do assigned tasks; and pulling the information together into one nice, neat, finished project.

The focus on easy collaboration in SharePoint Team Services shrinks the scale of major collaboration challenges by providing these new features:

- The new Shared Workspace enables you to see the list of people collaborating on the current project, find out who is online, and review tasks and other resources.

- The new Document Workspace appears as a task pane in Office applications and links you to the Document Workspace on the SharePoint Team Services site, where you can check documents in and out, review versions, discuss articles, and more.

- A new Meeting Workspace task pane, linked to a Meeting Workspace subnet created as part of your SharePoint Team Services site, enables you to organize, plan, discuss, and gather materials for upcoming meetings.

The sections that follow give you more information on each of these three collaboration features.

Working in a Shared Workspace

The Shared Workspace offers a kind of big-picture look at the collaborative documents and teams you're involved with. When you open the Tools menu and choose Shared Workspace (in Word, Excel, and Microsoft Office Power-Point 2003), the Shared Workspace task pane appears (see Figure 3-4) and provides information about the documents, team members, and resources you use when you work on collaborative documents.

Figure 3-4   The first time you use the Shared Workspace, you are prompted to create a new workspace area.

> **Tip**   You can also display the Shared Workspace task pane by clicking the Other Task Panes button (to the left of the task pane close box) and choosing Shared Workspace.

The Shared Workspace lists the members of your team and displays the active "pawn" icon beside those who are currently online. This is great when you need to send an instant message ("Would you please upload that new logo so that we can take a look before the meeting today?") and when you want to review the tasks you still need to do in advance of the meeting. The Shared

Workspace tools (which are also available in the Document Workspace) allow you to get more information about your shared files:

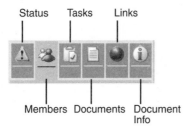

- Status tells you the current checked-in/checked-out status of the selected document.

- Members shows you who your collaborators are for the selected document and lets you know which of your team members are currently online.

- Tasks displays the current tasks assigned for this document and enables you to mark tasks as completed when you're finished with them.

- Documents provides the name and workspace for the current document.

- Links displays additional resources, folders, and files team members can access for more information.

- Document Information shows the author of the document, the name of the person who last modified it, and the date and time it was changed. Any document properties you set using SharePoint Team Services will also be visible in the Document Information tab.

Creating a Document Workspace

In addition to providing the workspace inside Office where team members can get helpful information about their collaborative projects, the Shared Workspace also allows you to create document workspaces for documents you want to share and then displays information in the task pane when you're working in the various Office applications.

> **Tip**   A document workspace is a Web site in SharePoint Team Services that enables you to collect, organize, view, modify, share, and discuss documents, spreadsheets, presentations, and more. You can create one or many document workspaces, depending on how many collaborative projects you're involved with; the Shared Workspaces task pane displays information relevant to your current document and lists the other documents in the same document library on SharePoint Team Services.

You can create a document workspace in several different ways:

- Display the Shared Workspace task pane in Word, Excel, or PowerPoint; enter a location for the new document workspace; and click Create.

- Send a document a "live" attachment to an Outlook e-mail message. The document is sent to all recipients of your e-mail message and also saved as a document workspace at the address you specify in the Create Document Workspace field. (For more about creating a live attachment, see "Working with Live Document Attachments" in the following section.)

- If you are using an Office application and want to save the file to your shared workspace, you can do so simply by choosing My Network Places on your local system or network drive. Choose the SharePoint site address from the Save in list, and click Save. The application saves the file in a document workspace and places it on the Share-Point Team Services site in the workspace area you selected.

- Create a document workspace subweb directly in SharePoint Team Services by selecting an uploaded document and choosing Create Workspace.

Each of these creation methods has its merits, and depending on where you spend the majority of your time (working in a specific Office application, e-mailing messages and documents, or browsing the Web), you might use one or all approaches for creating document workspaces while you work.

This seamless integration with Office applications allows users to save documents to an online document library as easily as they would to their own hard drive. With versioning and check-in/

check-out features enabled in SharePoint, you can ensure that individuals are always working with the (one and only) most current version of any given document.

Working with Live Document Attachments

Perhaps the easiest way to create a document workspace—especially if you spend a lot of time online—is to simply e-mail the latest version of a file to someone on your team. Now in Office 2003, when you use Outlook to send an e-mail with a file attachment, an Attachment Options button appears to the right of the Attach field. Click it to display the Attachment Options task pane, and choose one of the following:

- Regular attachment sends a static copy of the document on your hard drive to the recipient.

- Live Attachment sends the recipient a copy of the document you sent but also creates a new document workspace and stores a copy of the document there.

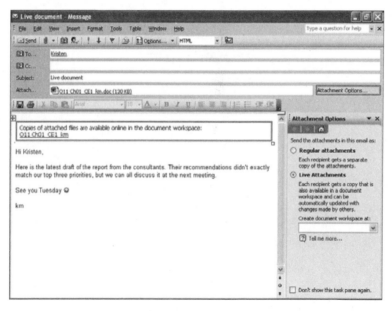

When you click Live Attachments, a message appears above the text in the body of your e-mail message, giving a link to the new document workspace created for the attached document.

A Look at a Document Workspace   The first time you click the link to go to the document workspace on SharePoint Team Services, you are greeted with an introductory page that tells you the URL for the site and provides some basic information about page components. Each document workspace includes three primary elements:

- A Document Library for collecting the collaborative document and supporting files, such as graphics, charts, spreadsheets, data tables, memos, and more

- A Task list that enables you to assign specific activities to different members of your team

- A Links list displaying resources team members can use as they do their part on the collaborative document

After you click OK, the document workspace is displayed. Figure 3-5 shows the default document workspace with the various default elements and the Quick Launch navigation bar.

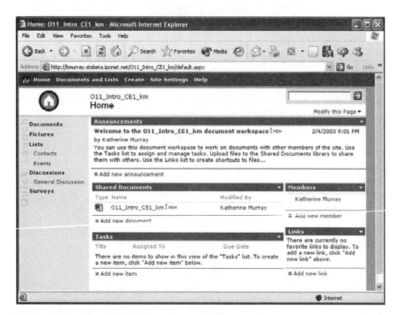

Figure 3-5   The default document workspace design provides space for announcements, tasks, members, links, and more.

Don't let the busy look of the document workspace fool you—you can customize this site with your own project-related information in just minutes, adding documents to the library, inviting members and setting permissions, adding links, and assigning tasks. The entire process can be completed in less than 10 minutes, and no matter how much information you need to share, you'll have a central point for managing documents and communication related to your team's project.

How Can You Use the Document Workspace?

If your Internet business is preparing to launch a new custom Web service for your subscribers, you can use the various elements in the document workspace to organize and share information in this way:

- In the Announcements area, you could let the group know about news items relevant to the new service.

- In Shared Documents, you can publish the latest specs on the new service, a document reporting on the current user survey results, the proposal and specifications of the software engineer working on the project, and the latest version of the documentation and marketing materials being prepared for the service.

- In the Members area, you can list the various team members working on the project (John, IT manager; Teresa, marketing; Phil, software designer; Terri, project manager; Paul, customer service).

- In the Tasks area, you can assign duties to each member. (Phil evaluates prototype 2 and reports back; Teresa gets production bids for the new promotional materials; John produces a timeline for the prelaunch and launch events; Paul completes his customer surveys and makes the results available online.)

- The Links area provides team members with Web pages, online documents, and additional sources of information (competitors' sites, results of recent Web research, software specification standards, project-management forms, links to graphic design and printing resources).

Whether you work in a software-related business, an insurance company, a Fortune-500 corporation, or a small town hall, you'll quickly grasp how using this type of list-based information in a collaborative environment can reduce the time you spend organizing people and agonizing over the details of data management in teams.

Uploading Documents   You can also upload files directly to your document workspace on SharePoint Team Services by logging on to your team site and clicking the Shared Documents header in your workspace site. In the Shared Documents library, you can click the Upload Document link to display an upload page. (See Figure 3-6.) Simply enter the name of the file you want to add to the library (or click Browse to navigate to the folder on your local drive), click Save, and click Close to upload the file and return to Shared Documents.

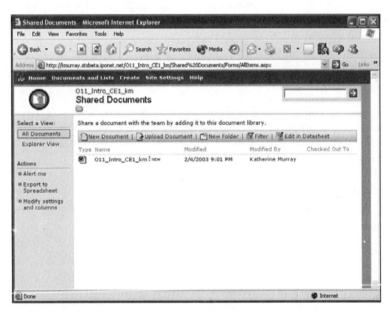

Figure 3-6   You can upload a document directly to your document workspace by clicking Upload Document in the Shared Documents library.

Because business users often need to upload not only a single file but a collection of files (for example, all files, notes, meeting minutes, and presentations related to the new HR benefits package your team is evaluating), SharePoint Team Services supports the uploading of multiple files as well. You can click the Upload Multiple link on the Upload Document page to display a

Windows Explorer–like list of folders and subfolders on the current drive. Click the folder you want, and select the check box to the left of the displayed documents to choose the files you want to upload; then click Save, and click Close to start the process.

Enhanced Document Library Features   Document libraries were a popular feature of SharePoint Team Services version 1, enabling team members to upload, store, and access developing documents and resources related to their specific projects. A software group might store research documents, test surveys, reviewer comments, and the developing documentation in a document library. An HR team might collect information from various benefits providers, contact information, proposals, sample client letters, proposal evaluations, and more. A team focused on planning a corporate annual meeting might store in their document library the various documents, presentations, and support notes that will be distributed at the meeting, as well as a planned agenda and participant list.

Using SharePoint and document workspaces, you can create multiple document and form libraries and customize them to fit the needs of your particular business. Document libraries house files related to your collaborative project and support great features for document management, including versioning (with which you can ensure that the most recent version of the file is in use) and check in/check out, which controls access to files so that only one user can modify a file at any given time.

Versioning   You can keep track of different copies of the same documents using the new versioning feature in SharePoint. After you've created and uploaded a document into a document library, you can track the various versions of the document and identify and remove outdated versions from the library. Versioning features are supported throughout SharePoint and in Word, Excel, and PowerPoint. The Shared Workspace pane also displays version information in the Information tab.

> **Note**   Versioning is disabled by default. To enable versioning, go to the document library you want to use, select the library, and click Modify settings and columns in the Actions section of the Quick Launch bar. Under General Settings, click Change general settings and scroll down to Document Versions. Click Yes to enable versioning, and click OK to save the change.

Document Check In and Check Out   Another new document-management feature in SharePoint is the check-in/check-out feature, which helps you make sure that no more than one person is working on a file at a time. You check out a document by clicking its context menu in the document library and choosing Check Out. When you check out a file, the file is copied to the server (or your standalone system), where you can work with it until you want to make it available through check in.

> **Tip**   Team members can find out whether a document is checked in or out on the Status tab of the Shared Workspace task pane.

When you want to check a document back in, return to the Document Library and click the document's down arrow. Choosing Check In prompts SharePoint to give you the option of returning the document to team view in the library, saving changes to the site but keeping the document checked out, or discarding your changes and undoing the check-out procedure. (See Figure 3-7.)

Figure 3-7   When you have revised a shared document, you can return it to the library by checking it in.

Web Discussions   If you've ever been the last recipient in a long list of reviewers for a specific document, you know how hard it is to read through everyone else's comments and add your own. Further, if you're working in a document with Track Changes enabled, your revisions might pile on enough comments that the document file crashes or is unreadable because of the dozens of balloons packed into the right margin.

Web discussions are now part of SharePoint Team Services, and they allow you and your teammates to review and discuss documents without actually making changes to the document file. No check in or check out required. To enable Web discussions on a particular document in your document workspace, simply click the down arrow for the document in the Shared Documents library; then choose Discuss from the context menu. The document is displayed in a reading pane, and the Discussions toolbar appears along the bottom of the viewing area. To add a comment, click New Comment; the Enter Discussion Text dialog box appears. (See Figure 3-8.) You can then enter a title and the text and click OK. Web discussion threads are saved independently of the document under review, so no changes are actually made to the document itself.

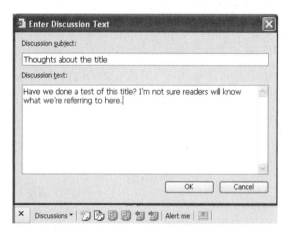

Figure 3-8   Web discussions enable you to comment on shared documents without making changes in the file.

The Discussions toolbar includes an Alert Me tool, which automatically creates an alert that lets you know when the document is changed, reviewed, or commented on in the future. Outlook coordinates the alerts along with SharePoint and receives e-mail messages notifying you of changes according to the frequency you specify.

> **More Info**   For more information on creating and managing alerts in SharePoint, see the section, "Setting SharePoint Alerts," later in this chapter.

Additional Document Workspace Features   Document workspaces in SharePoint Team Services offer many additional features that allow you to customize your sites to the goals and tone of your organization. You can choose to create moderated sites (unmoderated is the default), create new views that enable you to display your document libraries in new ways (with expanded field capability), customize the individual list components on your site by modifying the Web Parts on which they are based; apply different site templates and create your own; and ensure the security of your information by setting permissions and managing roles for specific documents.

Meeting Workspace

Another new collaboration feature in Office 2003 helps you gather and organize everything (and everyone) related to meetings. The Meeting Workspace is a Web site in SharePoint Team Services that provides the tools and space for coordinating documents, minutes, agendas, task lists, action items, discussions, and scheduling for your upcoming meeting. You might use the Meeting Workspace to:

- Collect product descriptions for the review board meeting and make them available in advance to participating members

- Discuss and review your development committee's new fundraising plan before you present it to the Executive Board

- Prepare notes, presentations, and marketing materials for your group presentation at the company meeting

- Organize, discuss, and revise a proposal packet to be presented to a new major client

Creating a New Meeting Workspace   You can create a new meeting workspace in two ways: through Outlook or directly on your SharePoint Team Services site. In Outlook, when you prepare to send a meeting request to others on your team (or in a new group not yet formed), you can click Meeting Workspace to start the process. The Meeting Workspace task pane opens on the right side of the request window. You can enter the name of the server on which the workspace will be stored, and click Create. (See Figure 3-9, on the next page.)

Figure 3-9 You can create a new meeting workspace when you send out meeting invitations in Outlook.

Linking to an Existing Workspace

If you've previously created a meeting workspace and you're ready to add a new meeting request as part of that meeting, both Outlook and SharePoint will keep track of your workspaces and enable you to link directly to an existing workspace. From Outlook, you can create a new meeting request that's part of an existing meeting workspace by clicking the Change settings link to display the Meeting Workspace settings pane. Click the Link To An Existing Workspace button, click the Select The Workspace down arrow, and then choose the existing meeting workspace from the list.

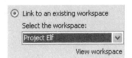

If you're unsure about the meeting workspace you've selected, you can verify that you've chosen the right one by clicking the View Workspace link. The meeting workspace you are linking to is displayed in your browser so that you can verify that you're hooking up with the right site.

If you're working on your SharePoint Team Services site, you can create a new meeting workspace when you set up a new event. Scroll to the Events section of your SharePoint main page, and click the Add a new event link. On the New Items page, enter event information (the title of the meeting, the start and end times, a brief description if needed, and so on); then select the Workspace check box to create a new meeting workspace. (See Figure 3-10.)

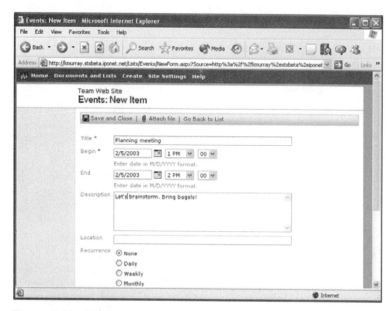

Figure 3-10   You can set up a new meeting workspace when you create an event in SharePoint Team Services.

After you click Save and click Close on the New Item page, you are taken to a page that enables you to create a new meeting workspace or link to an existing workspace. Enter the workspace title (the name of the event you just created is inserted by default), and fill in other pertinent information. You also have the option of setting user permissions for access to the meeting. (See the section "Setting User Permissions" for more about securing data on your SharePoint site.)

After you click OK, you can select one of six meeting workspace templates. Each template includes a different set of list items that you can use to organize the information, documents, and people involved with your meeting. Table 3-1, on the next page, introduces you to the different meeting workspace templates.

Table 3-1   Meeting Workspace Overview

Template	Lists	Description
Basic Meeting	Objectives Attendees Agenda Document Libraries Action Items Decisions	Use the Basic Meeting template to set up the structure for your meeting, store resource documents, assign tasks, and call for specific decisions.
Blank Workspace	No predefined lists	Choose Blank Workspace when you want to create your own workspace without any prefabricated fields. You might use Blank Workspace to create a simple list of events or customize the look by choosing different lists.
Decision Making	Objectives Attendees Agenda Document Libraries Action Items Decisions	The focus of the Decision Making template is on providing attendees with all the resources they need to come to a decision on specific items.
Social Gathering	Attendees Things To Bring Directions Discussions Picture Library	Social Gathering is a fun, informal meeting style that spotlights people, pictures, and conversation more than document review or sharing.
Training Session	Objectives Attendees Agenda Document Libraries Discussions	The Training Session template provides lists for managing people, schedules, documents, and discussions. No need for action items or decisions here.

Once you choose your meeting workspace template and click OK, the new meeting workspace site is displayed. You can now add the various list items by clicking the appropriate links and adding your own meeting information.

Setting User Permissions Security is a primary concern for many organizations that spend more and more time online. How can you be sure that only the people with access to your meeting documents are viewing them? Is there a way to secure the documents so that others can view but not modify them?

SharePoint Team Services uses a permissions-based system to allow varying degrees of access to all the activities on a SharePoint site. The same permissions system is used for shared workspaces, document workspaces, and meeting workspaces. When you first create a meeting workspace, you have the option of choosing which user group you want individuals to be assigned to. Different user groups are granted different levels of accessibility to the site. For example, you might allow some attendees full access to view, modify, upload, and delete documents, and you might want to limit other attendees to simply reading the materials posted online. The different user groups are as follows:

- Reader is given read-only access to the site. This means the participant can review all list items and read documents, but can't make any changes on the site or modify the documents in any way.

- Contributor (which is assigned to each attendee by default) can add content to existing document libraries and lists, delete items as needed, and create new subwebs.

- Web Designer can create new lists and document libraries and customize pages and Web Parts.

- Administrator has full control of the site and is able to set permissions, create and delete sites, and control all aspects of site management.

You can view and modify the permissions in any workspace in SharePoint Team Services by clicking Settings (in the top menu bar of the current page) and selecting Manage Users in the Administration area. To view and change permissions for a user, click the user name, and then click the Site Group to which you want to assign the user. (See Figure 3-11, on the next page.)

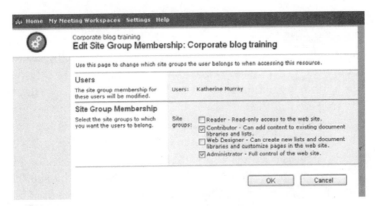

Figure 3-11   You can control the varying levels of access to workspace content by changing user group membership.

Tip   If you want to give participants access to your meeting without requiring permissions, you can select Allow Anonymous Access in the Language and Permissions area of the Settings page.

Managing Meetings

Once you get the hang of creating and using meeting workspaces, you'll be likely to prepare for all your major team meetings in this way. If you're like most of us, this means you'll quickly be creating a list of meetings in the future. How will you keep a handle on them all? SharePoint Team Services brings all your meeting workspaces together on the My Meetings Workspaces page, where you can create new meeting workspaces, go directly to other existing workspaces, or delete ones you no longer need.

You can access the My Meeting Workspaces page by clicking the link in the top menu bar of any Meeting Workspace.

Contacts and Communications

In Chapter 2, you learned about the new changes in Outlook that enable you to communicate instantly with others without leaving your Office applications. SharePoint Team Services offers a number of features that extend beyond the reach of Outlook, allowing you to sync both your calendar and your contacts with your local system and stay in touch with changes on your SharePoint Team Services sites by setting up e-mail alerts. When you sync both your calendar and contacts, you always have access to the most current scheduling and contact information. This section takes a closer look at all three of those shared features.

Sharing Calendar Events

You can easily add the events you schedule in your meeting workspace or on your SharePoint team Web site to your personal Outlook calendar. From Outlook, go to your Events page (click the Events heads on the main SharePoint team page) and click Link To Calendar. (See Figure 3-12, on the next page.) Outlook will display a message telling you that a request has been made to add a SharePoint Team Services folder to your Outlook calendars. Click Yes to continue, and the SharePoint Team Services calendar is added under Other Calendars. The new events are added to your Calendar in the current view. (See Figure 3-13, on the next page.)

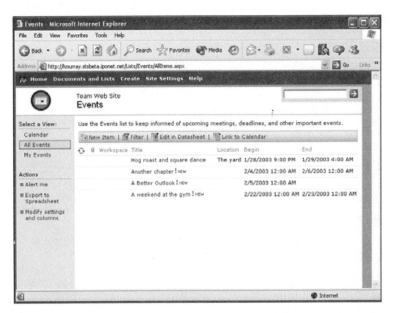

Figure 3-12   You can add your online events to your Outlook calendar by clicking Link To Calendar in SharePoint Team Services.

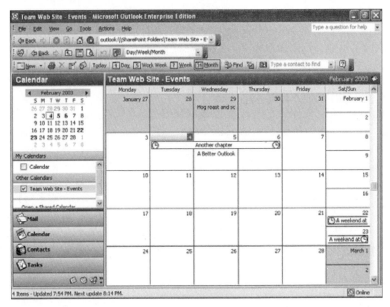

Figure 3-13   The events you created on the SharePoint site are added to your Outlook calendar.

Sharing Contacts

You can also share your Contacts in much the same way as you can your calendar events. From your SharePoint Team Services site, click Contacts in the Quick Launch area. To link your SharePoint Team contacts to your Outlook contacts, click Link To Contacts. Outlook alerts you that permission has been requested to add a SharePoints Team Services folder to Outlook. Click Yes to continue. The folder is added under Other Contacts in the Navigation Pane of your Outlook Contacts view.

You can also upload your Contacts list (or a group or individual in your Contacts list) to share with the team. To add contacts to the SharePoint list, click Import Contacts on the Contacts page. When the Select Users To Import dialog box appears, choose the names you want to import, and click Add; repeat as many times as needed, and click OK.

> **Note**   You can add information for people only you contact in My Contacts view to keep it separate from the contacts shared by the rest of the team. For example, suppose that it's your job to work with the writer, illustrator, and photographer for the corporate history project, but the rest of your team has no reason to contact them. You can add those contacts to your My Contacts view so that you can find them easily. To display that view, click the link under Select A View in the SharePoint Team Services page and then click Import Contacts to add users to your personal contact list.

Setting SharePoint Alerts

Throughout SharePoint Team Services, you can set alerts documents and activities so that you receive notification when items are added, changed, deleted, or discussed. (See Figure 3-14.) You also can set the frequency of alerts and determine whether you receive immediate, daily, or weekly summaries of changes in the library.

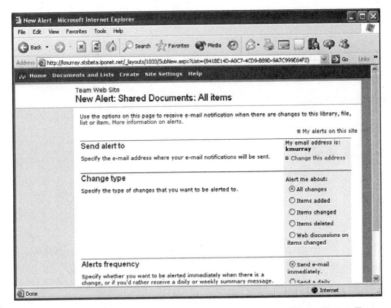

Figure 3-14   You can sign up for alerts on your SharePoint Team Services site so that you know when changes are made.

You might use alerts, for example, when you're working with time-sensitive material and need to make all changes by a certain date. Instead of checking the site each day to see whether a member has uploaded his or her portion of the document, you can assign an alert to the library so that when a new file is added, an automatic e-mail arrives in your Inbox telling you so. This leaves you free to worry about more pressing matters, while SharePoint and Outlook take care of keeping you up to date.

After you set up alerts, a message is delivered to your Inbox letting you know that the alert was created successfully. This is the type of message you'll receive when documents are added, removed, checked in, or discussed. Two links in the message always give you the option of accessing the team site to review the changes or going to the alerts-management page to review and modify your alert settings. (See Figure 3-15.)

Figure 3-15   E-mail alerts arrive in Outlook telling you about changes that have been made and providing links back to the document library and your alert-management settings.

Improved SharePoint Features

SharePoint Team Services version 1 provided a way to create a quick, smart solution to the challenge of organizing work teams both inside and outside organizations. In version 2 of SharePoint Team Services, a number of features have been added and improved to make site creation as simple and fast as possible, using out-of-the-box features users can customize later if they choose. Now, in SharePoint, you can literally create a meeting request, and in the time it takes you to fill out the form and click Send, you can create a new meeting workspace, using one of six predefined workspace templates.

In addition to the fast functionality and ease-of-use features, SharePoint Team Services now includes the following enhancements:

- New field types now include calculated columns that allow the use of formulas and expressions in lists.

- New and improved view options give you pre-designed views and enable you to create new views with columns and styles to match your specific categories.

■ A powerful new datasheet view provides a flexible and powerful filtering and sorting tool for list information and provides quick links to Excel and Access Word (See Figure 3-16).

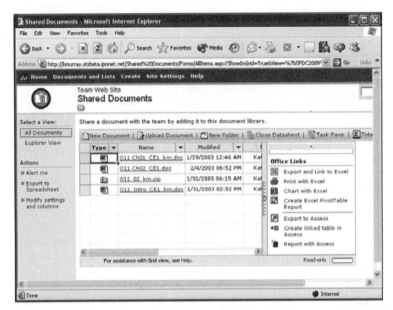

Figure 3-16 You can control the varying levels of access to workspace content by changing user group membership.

■ Filtering controls in document libraries enable you to display only files that meet specific criteria.

■ Photo libraries allow you to upload and view images related to your document or meeting workspace.

■ Developer tools and support for creating Web Parts and Smart Pages for businesses and organizations to use in conjunction with SharePoint Team Services. The inclusion of modifiable Web Parts opens up opportunities for designers, IT professionals, and third-party vendors to develop customized and subscription-based content for use in specific industry applications.

■   A new survey feature enables you to create online surveys to collect information from team members. By following a simple process, you can set up questions and choose response types that will give you the information you need. Participants can then take the survey online (see Figure 3-17, on the next page), and administrators can view, chart, and export survey results for use in other Office applications.

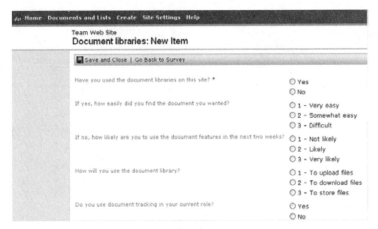

Figure 3-17   Create and use online surveys to gather important data about the projects you're managing.

Summary

This chapter has given you a first look at SharePoint Team Services version 2, providing ideas on how you can use the various features of the program and exploring how it extends the collaboration and communication features built into Office 2003. We've touched on the main characteristics of SharePoint here, but there's much more to discover. When you get the chance, explore on your own. As a key point in extending the collaborative nature of Office 2003, SharePoint Team Services enables you to bring people, ideas, and resources together in a new way to get your work done effectively, efficiently, and collaboratively.

4

Introduction to Microsoft Office OneNote 2003

W. Frederick Zimmerman

How many times have you scribbled a note on a napkin or doodled a chart on an envelope, misplaced it, and then wished you had it later? Have you ever had a conversation with a client and then wandered out to your car, desperately trying to retain the details of what was just said? Microsoft Office OneNote 2003 is an exciting new product that enables you to capture the best of your in-the-moment ideas and turn them into valid, usable information in real time. OneNote complements the core applications by giving you a way to capture, store, organize, and use research and support data in flexible new ways.

If you have your Tablet PC in a meeting, for example, you can use OneNote to sketch out the new organizational chart people might be having trouble grasping. You can project the chart onto a screen and use OneNote as a digital whiteboard for brainstorming sessions. If you're in a coffee shop, you can jot down a few reminder notes and then add them instantly to your Task list in Microsoft Office Outlook 2003. If you're in the car, you can use the audio feature to record and store a quick note or two; and with a single click, you can link the audio to your typed or handwritten notes about a client meeting so that you can be sure you've got all the information stored together in one place, where you can easily access it later. Wherever you are and however you work, if you have good ideas and a Tablet PC (or OneNote installed on your notebook computer or desktop system), you can put those ideas to work as real information right away.

If you do most of your note taking by typing on laptop or desktop systems, you can keep OneNote open on top of other applications, so you can capture, save, format, print, search, e-mail, and share your notes easily without getting sidetracked from your current task. (See Figure 4-1.) The power of the program is its flexibility—it works the way you do, encapsulating your thoughts in the way you're most comfortable recording and applying them.

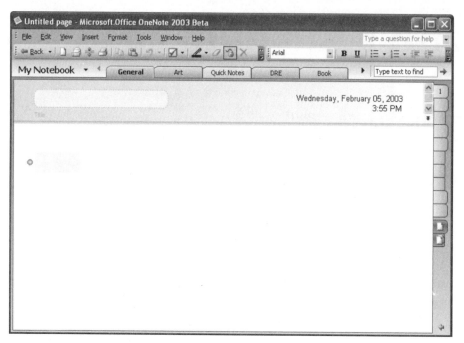

Figure 4-1   A 50,000-foot view of OneNote.

This chapter introduces you to OneNote and gives you a first look at the program's many features. You'll see why OneNote is considered a revolutionary new tool that will change the way we capture and work with information, enhancing the productivity of both individuals and enterprises.

From the Experts

Microsoft Office Product Manager Roan Kang is excited about the new possibilities OneNote offers: "In general, we see OneNote as the 'staging area' for capturing and organizing your thoughts and ideas prior to the creation of more formal documents. So it's not too hard to see every information worker in the future using OneNote to collect facts and research before creating their presentations and memos. Also, OneNote is a great way to make meetings and brainstorming sessions more productive. We can see someone easily taking notes during the course of a meeting, and organizing those notes to highlight crucial action items, and then sharing those notes with people who were both attending and those who were unable to make the meeting. More specifically, since OneNote is designed to work the way you want, we believe that different companies and organizations will be able to adapt OneNote to their specific needs in ways that we can't even imagine right now."

Why Is Improved Note-Taking Important?

Just visualize the notes for your last term paper or think about the last time someone handed you a list of phone messages. Research shows that most people have difficulty doing more than one thing at a time, even tasks as familiar as talking on a cell phone while driving. Note-taking—a process for understanding, summarizing, and organizing unfamiliar, complex, or difficult-to-remember material—can place considerable cognitive load on the brain when you're also trying to accomplish another task. Case in point: most people know how difficult it is to participate actively in a meeting and take notes at the same time.

According to a Microsoft survey, nearly 40 percent of employed U.S. adults reported that they wanted a more efficient way to take notes. According to Rob Newing in *Management Week*, a survey carried out by Microsoft Research found that 91 percent of us regularly take down handwritten notes, but only 26 percent of us transfer them to digital format, and 23 percent often can't find our notes in the first place.[1] It follows that there's room to make note-taking work better. Microsoft has developed software routines that electronically

---

1. http://www.vnunet.com/Analysis/1138445

ease much of the drudgery of note-taking and automate tasks that were impossible to do manually.

Why Is Improved Note-Taking Essential to Enterprises?

Because information is important to organizations, and using information effectively enhances productivity, OneNote can provide an excellent, easy-to-learn-and-use tool for capturing and sharing notes across a variety of media. Specifically, organizations can benefit in a number of ways by providing a flexible note-taking tool:

- Individuals will be more productive—and perhaps more accurate—in their work. Transfer this benefit incrementally across hundreds or thousands of information workers, and the result is a substantial gain in productivity.

- Teams will be more productive when their members are connected together.

- Communication among team members will be increased through shared notes.

- Relationships with clients will be enhanced given better follow-through on interviews and requests.

- Research and fact-gathering for team projects will be improved.

- Flexible note-taking will enable individuals to gather information in the way they are most comfortable, which translates to better information.

- Less duplication of effort will occur (taking notes by hand in a meeting and then typing them in a document afterward).

- Easy sharing of notes enables individuals to share and report on meetings, projects, and more, keeping others in the loop in real time.

What specific factors should an enterprise consider as it examines the return on investment of deploying OneNote? The cost and risk factors both appear relatively low. OneNote is a modest-size application, and its installation is pain-free. Because OneNote is closely related to Microsoft Office 2003, it gains the cost benefits of riding on the mature and strong security and ease-of-use features being added to Office.

What benefits make OneNote a "must do now" installation for an enterprise? OneNote can be particularly beneficial in certain organizations and for specific activities.

- **Project management**, whether on a small scale or large, is essential to almost every enterprise. Project management is about organizing work and accurately communicating its status. Microsoft Office Project 2003 is the standard for project-management, and it addresses most of the formal information needs of project managers. But project management also has an informal side, which is about quick meetings, brainstorming, problem-solving, and communication. As you'll learn later in the chapter, OneNote offers synchronized audio and digital whiteboarding, plus the advantage of mobility on a laptop or Tablet PC, so it can dramatically improve the efficiency with which project managers and project management teams carry out the informal side of their jobs.

- **Education and training** touches the IT staff in many enterprises. We all know from sitting through day-long passive presentations that they can be an inefficient use of everyone's time. The notes scribbled on training printouts are rarely useful and have no life expectancy. Getting trained at a computer can rapidly morph into checking e-mail (if the training computer is connected to the Internet) or playing solitaire (if it isn't). OneNote, with its friendly, intuitive options for data entry, offers a way to make note-taking a much more dynamic, constructive, and common part of at-work training.

- **Information technology and tech-support functions** are significant in most modern enterprises. OneNote helps IT and tech-support staffs plan their projects and processes more efficiently so that less time and money are spent in implementation. Steve McConnell's classic survey, *Rapid Development* (Microsoft Press, 1996), cites numerous peer-reviewed studies to confirm the adage that a day spent in design is worth a dozen spent in coding. Similarly, an error detected in testing is much more expensive to fix than those detected at earlier stages. OneNote will make careful preparation and design an enjoyable experience for your team.

■ **Sales** is the sine qua non of every enterprise, even non-profits. For any enterprise to survive, it must have people who go out and talk to customers and bring back a clear definition of customer needs. Capturing fast-moving informal conversations is exactly where OneNote shines. How much is it worth to get a customer's requests right, or avoid a blunder? How much is one major sale worth to your enterprise compared to the relatively modest cost of deploying OneNote on the front lines? Sales reps need a reliable mechanism for capturing and managing many tiny bits of information that are not necessarily suitable for inclusion in an enterprise's existing sales information system. OneNote lets a sales rep synchronize written notes with an audio recording of a conversation.

■ **Publishing and communications** organizations within enterprises might find OneNote a remarkably useful electronic publishing tool because it provides a completely intuitive page layout—mixing text, digital ink, graphics, and Web pages. OneNote gives informal e-publishers great control over the location of items on the page, but without requiring the specialized knowledge of page layout. OneNote is also very well suited for applications where the publisher wants to encourage active note-taking and reader response.

Why Improved Note-Taking Is Essential to Individuals

The quote from Stefan Smalla at the beginning of Chapter 1 articulates the "positive complexity" of the world we now live in. Simply put, we have a lot of information to track. The volume of data is empowering and, at times, overwhelming. Most information workers would gladly pay a modest sum to save a couple of hours a week by not having to retype notes, look for lost pieces of information, or make up for someone else's omission to carry out a crucial action item.

Beyond daily personal productivity, today's individual information workers pride themselves on *personal development*. The sobering truth is that in a rapidly globalizing world economy, you must be not only good at your job, but also the best fit for your job out of thousands of possible candidates, and there has to be no better way for your employer to achieve its goals than to continue to pay you. That means lifetime education is an ongoing personal responsibility for each of us…and note-taking is essential to learning. If there's an edge to be had in any aspect of continuing education, you need it—and that's what OneNote gives you.

Finally, individual note-taking is about *individual responsibility* and *personal accountability*. A big part of Microsoft's thinking in developing OneNote is to remove the barriers that prevent us from easily capturing information. As you'll learn later in the chapter, Microsoft has provided features in OneNote that specifically help capture information and follow up on it. It's about giving ourselves the tools that we need to remember our obligations, fulfill our responsibilities, and ensure that we do what we say we'll do, when we say we'll do it.OneNote can help make all of this possible.

For all these reasons, individual information workers should investigate OneNote as a revolutionary tool for personal empowerment.

Creating Notes

To start taking notes, open the OneNote application. OneNote affords the same great flexibility that you do get when you launch any other Windows application such as Word or Notepad. You can open OneNote in all the following ways:

■   Double-click the OneNote program icon or the OneNote shortcut on the desktop. (See Figure 4-2.)

Figure 4-2   The OneNote program icon.

■   Click Start, point to All Programs, point to Microsoft Office, and then click Microsoft OneNote.

■   Double-click any OneNote file to open a section of your notes. (OneNote files are indicated by the .one file extension, and they're stored by default in the My Notebook folder, although you can store them anywhere you like.)

■   Click the OneNote icon in the Windows system tray. This action launches OneNote in a small-screen view with all same functionality that is always available in OneNote. (See Figure 4-3, on the next page.) The small-screen view is handy for making quick notes while you're in the middle of another task, especially because the Quick Pane can be "pinned" to the top of your stack of open windows.

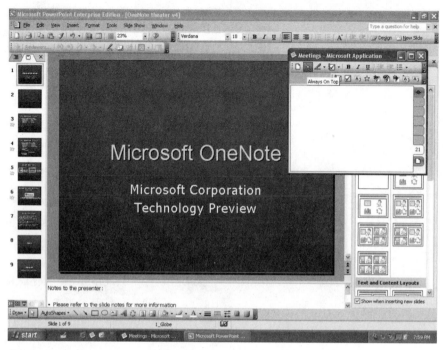

Figure 4-3   The OneNote Quick Pane.

How Does OneNote Fit with the Microsoft Office 2003 System?

- OneNote can be installed together with Office 2003 but does not require Office 2003 to function. You can use it with Office 2003 or as a completely standalone application.

- You can create tasks in OneNote and manage them with the Tasks feature in Microsoft Office Outlook 2003.

- You can save documents in OneNote in HTML so that they can be read easily by anyone with a browser, and you can cut and paste to and from Office 2003 documents into OneNote.

(continued)

How Does OneNote Fit with the Microsoft Office 2003 System?   *(continued)*

- OneNote is different from the current Office 2003 applications (Microsoft Office Word 2003, Microsoft Office PowerPoint 2003, Microsoft Office Excel 2003) in that instead of being used primarily to create "work product," it is totally focused on helping the user gather and manage information during informal and preliminary activities such as meetings, research, and conversations.

- OneNote is different from current Windows utilities such as Notepad in that it supports multimedia note-taking and has a much broader set of features.

- Most importantly, OneNote and Office 2003 share some of the same goals:

   - **Overcoming information fatigue.** OneNote helps you capture information in multiple formats and media and then organize it in a way that makes sense to you. This makes it easier for you to act on relevant information at the moment you acquire it.

   - **Improving collaboration.** OneNote aids such "blocking and tackling" aspects of collaboration as capturing meeting notes and generating follow-up actions.

   - **Encouraging appropriate use of productivity applications.** OneNote frees users from the difficulty of taking fast, simple, clear notes in applications that were designed to create complex final work products. OneNote is built from the ground up to support the note-taking task, and it serves as a "staging area" for organizing your notes and ideas before creating more formal documents.

Getting Started with Your Notebook

Just as buying three-tab, spiral-bound, college-ruled notebooks is a familiar ritual marking the beginning of every school year, setting up a new computer program requires certain set tasks for many information workers. Installing and setting up OneNote is easy—no trips to the office supply store! During installation, you'll be prompted for your name and organizational affiliation. (See the section "Installation" later in this chapter for more information on installing OneNote.)

Your OneNote "notebook" comes with a few sections already labeled, such as Quick Notes, and you can easily label and add sections yourself as you proceed. Each section corresponds to a .one file. (See Figure 4-4.)

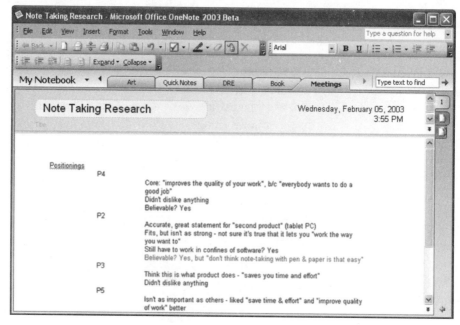

Figure 4-4   Notebook sections

The following topics describe the most useful features of OneNote and take you on a tour of the OneNote window.

Take Advantage of the Title Area

When we take notes on paper, we often scribble madly for a few minutes and then "catch up" during a momentary lull by adding procedural information such as the date, time, location, and subject of the note. Whether you write or type, OneNote gives you the flexibility to dive right into heavy-duty note-taking, or to enter the procedural information first. Here are some examples of the ways OneNote eases and personalizes the process of identifying your notes:

- OneNote divides the page into a title area and an input area.

- The title pane does not scroll with the rest of the page, like the navigational frames in many Web pages.

- The date and time are provided automatically by the program.

- You can enter any content you like in the title area: keyboard text, digital ink, or graphics and pictures. For example, a company might want to add its corporate logo to the title area.

- You can use basic text-formatting features similar to those in Word— font colors, bold, italic, and underline—as well as spell-checking and an Autocorrect feature that automatically detects and fixes common typos.

Put Notes Where You Need Them

As you begin entering notes, you'll notice that the OneNote page behaves differently from the familiar Word document in a crucial way; in a Word document, you can insert text only at the cursor location, and the cursor location can appear only where there is a line of text. For example, if you've just started a document, you can't type at the bottom of the page until your content reaches the bottom of the page. (See Figure 4-5.)

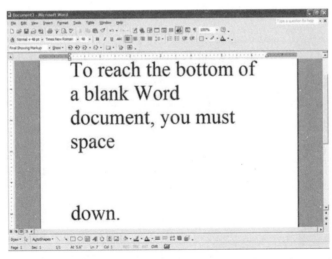

Figure 4-5   The traditional page metaphor in Word. You can insert text only where you've already created a paragraph, line, or table.

OneNote, on the other hand, behaves just like a piece of paper. You can put the cursor anywhere on the page to insert typed text, ink, or graphics. In Figure 4-6, text was placed in the bottom right without the need for such time-consuming tricks as creating hidden table cells or adjusting paragraph left margins. OneNote even offers *note handles* that let you drag chunks of notes anywhere you want them.

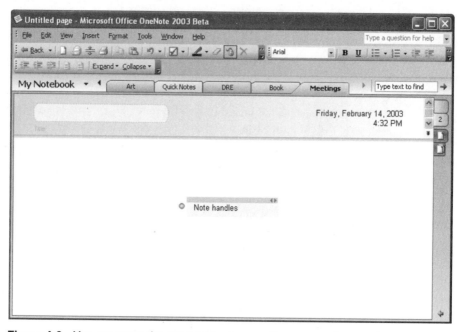

Figure 4-6   You can move the cursor anywhere on the page surface and start typing immediately, just like on paper.

The flexible 2-D page surface with note handles is a huge benefit to you and your enterprise for several reasons.

■   **OneNote removes a major source of mechanical delay.**   One of the principal reasons classic word processing software isn't optimized for taking notes is that capturing anything more than linear text notes entails time-consuming and frustrating formatting. Even saving a file requires answering questions about what to name it and where to put it. (Automatic saving is discussed further in the next section.)

- **OneNote works the way you work.**   In taking notes, many people like to use location as a way to organize and relate information. OneNote makes it easy and quick to put related pieces of information next to one another.

- **OneNote provides team members with a digital whiteboard for quickly capturing ideas.**   The information on the whiteboard can subsequently be shared via print, e-mail, file transfer, file shares, or Microsoft SharePoint Team Services sites.

Save Everything Automatically

There's no need to save your notes or transcribe the whiteboard at the end of a meeting, because everything you enter in OneNote is saved automatically. No decision making about when to use the Save command is required, meaning you won't miss something important while you take time to figure out what to name a file and where to save itNotes are saved by default in the My Notebook folder, so you'll always know where to look for them later. The goal of OneNote is to give you the same sense of security as paper: once you write it down, it's there.

Outline Your Notes

When you take notes in outline or bulleted form, OneNote provides the appropriate formatting. When you use the note handles to drag and drop a list near another list, the first list will be instantly merged with the second. Remember that just about every educational curriculum is organized in outline format, and almost every well-run meeting results in bulleted lists of information shared, decisions taken, and actions assigned. Because OneNote's outlining features do this formatting for you, you and your team will almost certainly be more productive.

Store Your Web Research in OneNote

Information workers use the Web to research both work-related topics (competitor data, continuing education) and personal topics (hobbies, weather, airline fares). Information gathered from Web research is often presented using HTML formatting that makes the page look good, but it's difficult to transfer the information into a tool such as a word processor or spreadsheet. OneNote solves this problem by seamlessly accepting Web pages, complete with graphics, into the same note area as text and ink. OneNote even brings along the Web address, and the hyperlinks in the pasted page still work—it's like a colorful, interactive scrapbook kept for you by a meticulous record-keeper!

To further clarify the benefits of inserting Web pages and graphics in your notes, ask yourself whether it's easier to remember that Tahiti is located at 15° 00S, 140° 00W and that the average temperature in February is 80° F, or is it easier to remember the image on the left side of the note shown in Figure 4-7?

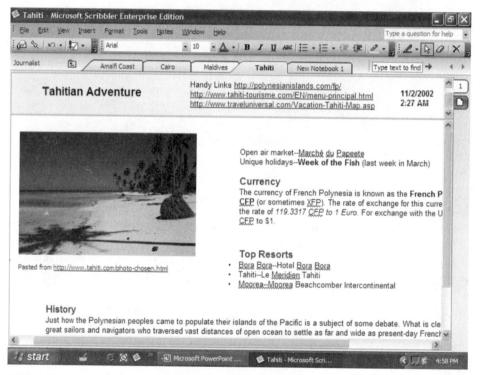

Figure 4-7 You can capture this image of Tahiti in OneNote.

For many people, it's much easier to remember a vivid picture. OneNote gives all of us the gift of visual note-taking!

The OneNote Research Pane

OneNote also includes the Office 2003 Research Pane and service, which allows you to search your intranet portals, the Internet, news services such as Factiva, encyclopedias, dictionaries, and other sources of information your organization might provide access to. You can take information you find through the research pane and add it to the growing collection you keep in OneNote.

Copying and Pasting To and From Other Office Applications

OneNote makes it easy to capture information from other applications for your notes. You can also copy and paste information from other Office applications by using the drag-and-drop feature within OneNote. Simply point to or select the desired information with the pointer, and then move it to any page in your notes. Items that can be moved into OneNote using the drag-and-drop feature include pictures and text from Web sites and Microsoft Word documents, slides from Microsoft PowerPoint presentations, and columns and rows of numbers from Microsoft Excel sheets.

Transferring information from your notes to other applications is also simple, as OneNote enables you to copy and paste information easily to other Office applications using the clipboard. When you copy and paste handwritten digital ink notes created in OneNote on a Tablet PC into other applications, the handwriting is automatically converted to text. Drawings are pasted as picture files.

Assign Note Flags

OneNote allows you to use *note flags* to assign any part of a note to a particular category, such as Follow Up, Idea, Important, Phone Number, or even Movies To See or CDs To Buy. You can create up to nine categories and customize their names, icons, and appearance. As note flags accumulate in OneNote, you can display a *Note Flags Summary pane* (shown in Figure 4-8, on the next page) where you can display, sort, and summarize note flags by category from any of your open notebook sections. If you're a fan of Tasks in Outlook, any OneNote note flags you've been using to represent to-dos can be moved to Outlook 2003 so that you can manage them there

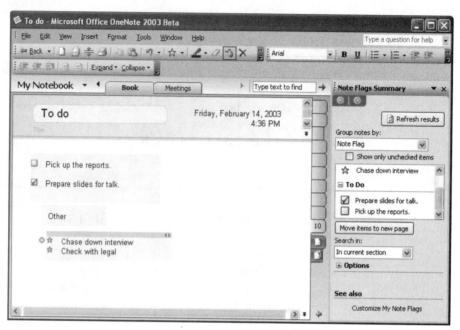

Figure 4-8   The Note Flags Summary pane.

By summarizing all your Follow-Up flagged note items, OneNote can give you an instant to-do list. By running through all your Idea flagged note items, OneNote can give you an instant brainstorming list. By recapping all your Buzzword Bingo custom flagged items, OneNote can give you an instant winner.

Break Your Notes into Pages

When a notebook section contains extensive outlined notes, complete Web pages, and striking graphics, it's easy to imagine that it could rapidly become quite cumbersome if it were a typical word processor document. Remember, the average school notebook contains 100 or so pages per subject. Fortunately, OneNote lets you break notes into pages and then organize them using the *page tab* feature, shown in Figure 4-9.

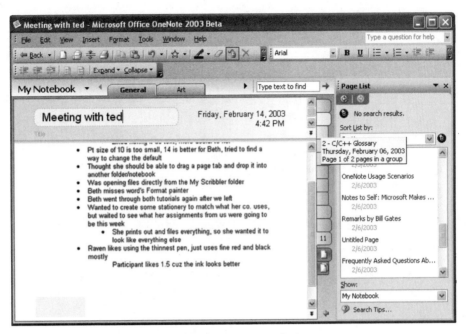

Figure 4-9   Use the OneNote page tabs to easily find your notes on a particular subject.

When you hover the pointer over a particular *page tab*, the page title and the date on which it was created is displayed. You can also use a button at the bottom of the page tab area (not visible in Figure 4-9) that widens the page tab area and shows you the titles of the pages in the page tabs. You can riffle through the pages of a notebook section by holding down the cursor and dragging it across all the page tabs. (*Riffling* is simply flipping through the page of your notebook until you find what you want.) You can then navigate straight to the page you want by clicking on the appropriate page tab. This is helpful because many people recognize their notes by how they look, not by their location or title. You can also create *page groups* in which all pages within the group contain the same information in the title area. And you can reorder pages in a group or in a notebook simply by dragging them to the desired location.

Personalize Your Notes Using Stationery

OneNote allows you to pick the stationery to use for your pages. Each section can use different stationery, and you can create your own—or even download it from the Microsoft Web site for Office (*www.office.microsoft.com*).

Keep Track of Your Note-Taking History

During a OneNote session, the program keeps track of all the pages you've visited recently. You can return to those pages by using the Back and Forward buttons, as in a browser.

Find Your Notes Using Keywords

You can use the Find box, which is located on the navigational toolbar and looks like the small Find boxes in Outlook, to search for keywords across all your notes in any open notebook sections. Pages containing results are highlighted in the page tabs area, and a sortable list of results is displayed in the rightmost pane, just like hits in a Web browser search. Similar to a Web browser search, the search results are linked to the actual notes, so jumping from your search results to the correct note is quick and easy.

The More Notes You Accumulate, the More OneNote Helps

The importance of the page flip, history, and find features increases in direct proportion as you accumulate a substantial body of notes. This means OneNote will give you the most navigational help at the end of the semester—near exam time—or when it comes time to write a major report for work, or when a project has generated many complex issues. OneNote comes through when you need it most.

Share Notes with Friends and Colleagues

When you reach the end of a note-taking session (or even before), you might want to share your notes with colleagues. You can accomplish this in several ways.

- **Send e-mail notes via Outlook 2003 as HTML e-mail and .one attachments.** OneNote is connected with Outlook 2003 so that you can send notes in a single step by clicking the envelope icon in the OneNote toolbar. The notes are mailed as HTML in the message body, so they are readable by anyone who has a mail client set to read HTML mail or a Web browser. Any ink or graphics included in the note will be included in the HTML as pictures.

Outlook 2003 also includes the note as an attached .one file, and any recipient who has OneNote installed can easily add that page to her own notebook simply by double-clicking the attachment. Imagine being able to share notes with a study group using a single e-mail!

Put Your Trip Reports on Hyperspeed

If you travel for work, you're probably all too familiar with the ritual of the trip report—the detailed summary of a business-related visit, usually created at considerable effort a few days after getting back from a tiring trip. Imagine that the moment your last meeting ends, you use offline or wireless e-mail to send your trip report out as a .one file. Again, Microsoft has raised the bar...you'll be working faster, better, smarter.

- **Send .one notes as attachments using older versions of Outlook.**   If you're using an older version of Outlook or another mail client, you can send .one files as attachments in just the same way that you send Word, PowerPoint, or any other data files. It is also easy to copy and paste to any mail message; the note content is pasted as HTML.

- **Publish notes as HTML.**   You can save your notes as HTML, which gives you great flexibility—you can e-mail them as attachments, or put the notes on a file share, a Web server, or a Microsoft Windows SharePoint Team Services site.

- **Collaborate with others using a file share or Windows SharePoint Team Services.**   You can save a section of your notes to a file share, or SharePoint Team Services site. A shortcut to that section then appears in your section tabs, and that section acts just like part of your notebook. Other users can then open that file from the shared location, and the same file is added to their notebooks. In this way, each person can add thoughts and research to this shared section so that over time it becomes a group notebook, or log. If the file is shared using SharePoint Team Services when you are working on it OneNote also shows the *shared workspace* pane, which indicates which other members of the shared workspace are online, what documents are related to this shared notebook, and so on.

Print Your Notes

Printed paper will continue to be an important part of the whole process of reviewing notes that you've taken, and OneNote gives you the same printing flexibility as other Microsoft applications.

■ You can print entire notebook sections, particular page groups, or individual pages. Imagine printing yesterday's notes every time you prepare for class.

■ You can show only certain levels of an outline and then print just those levels—handy for giving you an instant "table of contents" or "review guide" for a body of notes. Imagine printing out a list of all the issues that a project team has encountered and discussed, and then using the electronic copy on your laptop to closely examine the ones that are still problematic.

Publish Your Documents Electronically

OneNote is extremely well suited to electronic publishing of particularly visual or highly instructional visuals. A professor could prepare curricular material—say, an anatomy course—in OneNote files and then distribute it to students electronically. Students could then take advantage of the flexible 2-D page surface to annotate the notes either via standard keyboard input or digital ink. Since URLs within a OneNote page are active, it would be easy to create links from the curriculum to Web-based research services.

Finally, OneNote can bridge the gap to other electronic publishing media by saving a file as HTML. The file can then be opened in Word and saved in a variety of formats, including Rich Text Format (RTF), or as a .LIT file using Microsoft Read in Microsoft Reader plug-in.

Take Advantage of Extra Hardware

OneNote also contains features that make great use of extra hardware, such as a microphone or Tablet PC. While this hardware is not necessary to run OneNote, it can make your note-taking even easier and more productive. (See the section "System Requirements" later in this chapter for a complete list of the requirements for OneNote.)

Use a Microphone to Record Linked Audio   If your computer is equipped with a microphone, you can use OneNote's *record* feature to record audio as you take notes. The audio is linked to and synchronized with your notes so that you can re-create what was being said in a room while you were taking notes. Imagine the benefits of OneNote in the following scenarios:

- A program manager going back to his notes to find the place in his audio where someone made a commitment to an action item.

- A patient going back to his notes to play back his doctor's exact words.

- An attorney going straight to the place in a deposition where a damaging comment was made, and playing it back for the judge.

- A financial analyst replaying the teleconference he heard at his desk to catch the exact figures mentioned.

> **Note**   This feature does require that the audio be intelligible in the first place. If your PC does not have a high-quality built-in microphone, an external microphone is a good idea. OneNote simply marks the time and date that each note input was made and associates it with the audio feed saved at the same time. There is no "error-prone translation" or conversion from audio to text.

This feature lets you make your interactions more accurate and more accountable.

Tablet PC   If you have a Tablet PC, you can write and draw with digital ink just as you do in Tablet PC applications like Windows Journal. You can adjust the color and thickness of the ink, and you can put it anywhere you want on the page.

OneNote provides *writing guides*, shown in Figure 4-10, on the next page, that help the user write in a straight line and most especially build up structured notes bullet by bullet. Many of us have some difficulty writing many straight lines on unruled paper; writing guides help you keep your notes neat. Writing along a straight baseline also helps the computer understand your writing if you choose to apply Tablet PC's optional handwriting-recognition routines, which convert ink to plain ASCII text.

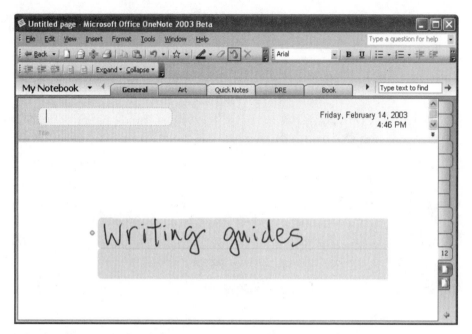

Figure 4-10 Writing Guides make it easy to write in a straight line.

Note that Tablet PC's handwriting recognition is entirely optional, and you might choose to keep your notes in ink format, just like paper notes that you simply refer to and don't bother to retype. Since the search functionality and other features of OneNote work equally well with text or ink, there's no need to convert everything you write to text. It's not the kind of handwriting recognition that you have to train. The basic guideline is that you use digital ink just like you use regular ink. If you use handwriting in your paper notes, you'll probably use handwriting in your digital notes.

> **Note** As in Windows Journal, there is a tool for inserting and removing spaces that you can use to make room for more inked notes or to close up gaps in a page.

This set of features deployed on the innovative Tablet PC platform works incredibly well for some applications, like student note-taking. (See Figure 4-11.)

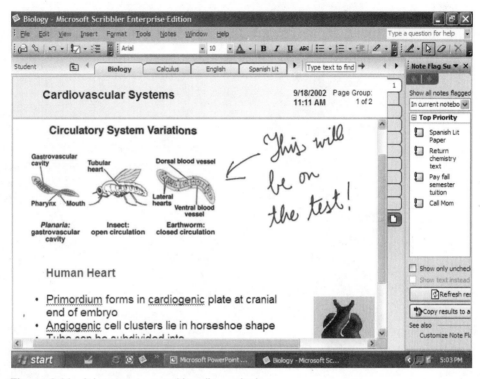

Figure 4-11   Ink notes on a multimedia curriculum.

System Requirements

Here are the system requirements for installing and running Microsoft OneNote:

■ A personal computer with a Pentium 133 MHz or higher processor. Pentium III is the minimum recommended for Windows XP.

■ Microsoft Windows 2000 Service Pack 3, or Microsoft Windows XP or later operating system.

■ 64 MB of RAM, plus an additional 8 MB of RAM for each application that you plan to run simultaneously. Since you'll often be running OneNote in parallel with other applications such as Office, Internet Explorer, and so on, we simply recommend 128 MB.

■ Installation of OneNote without Microsoft Office Professional 2003 requires approximately 70 MB of available hard disk space where the operating system is installed. If you already have Office Professional 2003 installed, OneNote will only add approximately

10 MB more to the size of Office Professional 2003. Please note that these figures are based on beta trials and may change for the final released version of OneNote.

■ A CD-ROM drive from which to install the software.

The following are *not* required:

■ **Office 2003.** Although OneNote will be released around the same time as Office 2003 and complements it very well, it does *not* require the latest version of Office to run, nor does Office 2003 require OneNote. OneNote does have certain advanced integration features, such as the ability to e-mail notes with one click, that do require Office 2003.

■ **Tablet PC.** Although OneNote works very well on a Tablet PC, you do *not* need a Tablet PC to run OneNote. Tablet PC *does* allow you to use digital ink in notes, which is a very important benefit, so if you can acquire a Tablet PC to run OneNote, by all means do so!

> **Tip**　More information on OneNote is available at *http://www.microsoft.com/office/onenote*.

Installation

When you acquire a new computer, especially if you are an enterprise user, Office and OneNote might already be installed. Installing OneNote on a computer that you already have is a straightforward experience similar to installing any other modest-size Microsoft application. If you install OneNote in an enterprise, you can use all the same powerful Windows and Office tools that you use today to install software over your internal LAN. Bottom line: this is an easy install!

From the Experts

Will future releases of OneNote offer possibilities for developers? Here's what Microsoft Office Product Manager Roan Kang had to say: "In OneNote Version 1.0, we were focused on making the product a great note-taking and management program, and as a result, it does not have any APIs. We are very eager to hear from the developer community to see what types of integration and solutions scenarios they are interested in developing with OneNote, and will definitely take that feedback into account for future versions. (In the meantime, of course, developers have a great note-taking and note-management program for their own notes and ideas.)"

The Future of OneNote

While Office 2003 is a powerful extension of one of the most feature-rich and mature applications of all time, OneNote is the introduction of a totally new type of application. This means that although OneNote will continue to be closely linked to future versions of Office, it will also have a trajectory of its own consistent with the typical growth of a 1.0 product. There are no firm plans defining future releases, but it seems reasonable to hope that Microsoft will round out the feature set with ease-of-use tweaks responding to user reaction to version 1; features for the developer community such as APIs and XML data structures; and integration extended to other applications such as Microsoft Project. Because OneNote runs especially well on the Tablet PC platform, it's also a good guess that as time goes by OneNote will add new Tablet-oriented features. Finally, it is reasonable to expect that we will see new features for user communities in which OneNote is especially well received.

Summary

This chapter has given you a first look at Microsoft OneNote, a flexible and functional (and fun) tool that complements the work you do in the core Office applications. By enabling you to capture, store, organize, and manage ideas in real time, OneNote helps you ensure that nothing important slips through the cracks in your busy, information-packed workday.

5

Support for XML

The enhanced system-wide support for XML (Extensible Markup Language) in Microsoft Office 2003 is one of the biggest and most exciting changes this new release has to offer. In alignment with the collaboration and extended communication focus of Office 2003, XML enables you to use your data more flexibly and store it in such a way that it can be used across platforms, countries, and just about any data barrier you can imagine. Do you have gigabytes of data locked away in old legacy systems that are inaccessible by today's software? Are there reports, legal briefings, analyses, and other documents saved on desktop PCs all over your organization that might offer some valuable data if you could find a way to pull them all together into a usable form?

XML—and its widespread support throughout Office 2003—can change all that. In this chapter, you'll learn how XML can improve what you do with data today and find out how the various XML features in Office 2003 will help you give your data a wider reach, a longer life, and enhanced value in your organization.

> **Note** This chapter focuses on the big picture of XML support in Office 2003 and details specific features in each of the core applications. Chapter 6, "XML Applied: Smart Documents, Smart Tags, and Microsoft Office InfoPath 2003," explores how XML is put into practice in these new, enhanced, programmable features of Office 2003.

The Power of XML

Imagine this: Two companies compete for a similar client base in a mid-size town in the Midwest. The companies are similar in size and offer similar products; but they differ greatly in their use of technology. The first company relies on a standard method for information exchange—when a department manager in sales wants to know the status of a product in development, she sends the product development manager an e-mail message: "Will product #2310 be available on the 15th as scheduled?"

Depending on how busy the product development manager is, he might or might not get right back to her. She waits for the information. Her potential customer waits for the information. She calls the manager but gets no answer. She walks down the hall (or across campus) to see whether she can find out more. Until the manager is able to respond to the question personally, everybody waits.

The other company uses XML as a data-exchange standard, allowing employees and managers to continuously update and draw information from databases and display it in user applications. All the information about the new product is stored in a database in XML format, so people with access to that information are able to pull it from the database as needed for use in reports, e-mails, tables, and spreadsheets. As a part of their sign-off process at the end of each business day, all department managers fill in a smart form based on InfoPath that enables them to enter quickly any status changes in the project. The information is saved in XML and deposited in a larger database. A combined status report is then generated automatically and delivered to each division supervisor for review. In this company, a sales manager wanting to know the status of the product (assuming she has access to this information in the database) has only to call up the product information in the database to answer the question—and pull together some real facts—for her waiting customer.

> **Note**   XML is about more than simple data storage—it's about the flexible way you can name your own data, save it independent of its form, and reuse and rebuild it in any number of different ways. The XML support built into Office 2003 allows users to work with the familiar Office interface and create and save documents as XML, without ever knowing they're actually working with XML. This means users need little or no additional training, can work with procedures similar to the ones they're familiar with, and ultimately save valuable data in a form that enables businesses to work smarter, faster, and more productively.

XML Basics

Even though you can use the XML features in Microsoft Office Word, Excel, and Access 2003 without knowing much about the technology or ever writing a single line of XML code, knowing the basics of XML can help you envision how it might be helpful in your own business. Toward that end, this section gives you some XML fundamentals and provides references for more information, in case you want to learn more or try a little coding yourself.

The Big Picture

Although it's hard to pin XML down to a concise definition, according to the easiest and broadest approach, XML is a highly flexible format for data exchange and application. In the big picture, users work with an Office 2003 document (Word, Excel, or Access) and attach an XML Schema (the set of rules determining the language elements used in the document). When they save the document, they can save it as an XML file and choose whether to save the data only or apply a transform (XSLT) to display the saved XML document in a specific view.

XML Glossary

Even though this chapter focuses on giving you an overview of XML and how it can be used to help streamline and extend the use of data in your organization, it's helpful to know the language. Here are some basic XML terms you're sure to see in this chapter and in other writings on XML:

- **DTD (document type definition).**   A set of rules that stores element names and attributes and defines how they can be combined and in which order.

- **Element.**   Any item defined in an XML document, enclosed with start and end tags: for example, <TITLE>First Look Microsoft Office 2003</TITLE>.

- **Style sheet.**   A collection of formatting instructions that control the display of the document. Style sheets can be in a separate file and linked to the document or housed in the document itself. (General recommendations are to store the data and style sheet separately, however, so the data can be used in its pure form in a variety of applications.)

(continued)

XML Glossary   *(continued)*

- **XML data.** Also called an *XML document*, the .xml file is the raw XML data stored independently of the way in which it is presented.

- **XML schema.** A document that defines the elements, entities, and content allowed in the document.

- **XSL (Extensible Stylesheet Language).** A language used to create style sheets that can be attached to XML documents to present the data in various forms.

- **XSLT (XSL Transformations).** Transforms the structure of an XML document to create different views.

More Than Markup

Some people refer to XML as a markup language because, after all, that's what its name (Extensible Markup Language) implies. But XML is more than a language of tags; it actually allows users to create their own markup languages specific to their data needs, based on a collection of set standards. With XML, you use specific rules to create your own tags and style sheets; the individual tags describe the content and meaning of the data rather than the display format of the data (which is what HTML controls). XML is generally reader-friendly, meaning that humans can easily read and follow the basic logic in the code. The following is a simple example of an XML document containing information about a series of workshops offered by a sporting goods company:

```
\*****************************************************************
<TRAINING>
    <CLASS>
        <TITLE>Mountain Biking</TITLE>
        <INSTRUCTOR>Lee</INSTRUCTOR>
        <DATE>August 8, 2003</DATE>
        <DURATION>6 weeks</DURATION>
        <COST>$240</COST>
    </CLASS>
    <CLASS>
        <TITLE>Rappelling</TITLE>
        <INSTRUCTOR>Jack</INSTRUCTOR>
        <DATE>June 24, 2003</DATE>
        <DURATION>4 weeks</DURATION>
        <COST>$160</COST>
    </CLASS>
    <CLASS>
        <TITLE>Kayaking</TITLE>
        <INSTRUCTOR>Jason</INSTRUCTOR>
        <DATE>July 10, 2003</DATE>
        <DURATION>6 weeks</DURATION>
        <COST>$240</COST>
    </CLASS>
</TRAINING>
*****************************************************************/
```

As you can see, each element has an opening tag and a closing tag (for example, the cost of a class is enclosed with a beginning <COST> and ending </COST> tag. The tagged elements are nested inside other tags; for example, each class record begins and ends with a <CLASS> tag; inside those tags, additional tags are nested for each of the individual data items stored for that particular class.

Because XML allows you to describe the content of the data, you can use that class information as easily in a database as you can in a spreadsheet, a word-processing document, a report, or an e-mail. Using an XML schema, which tells the document it's attached to how to read and apply the XML data, you can make XML data usable in many different forms in all sorts of different areas, from one end of your organization to the other.

On the other hand, HTML, the primary markup language used on the Web, is a tagging system that controls the way information is displayed. Headings, for example, might have an <H1> or <H2> tag to designate the size of the heading; the <FONT> tag might be used to specify the type family, size, color, and style of the text. But the HTML tags don't have any way of describing the content of the heading, and it's the content—the actual data itself—that can be used in other documents (databases, spreadsheets, reports, and so forth). That's what XML data does.

Data Here, Format There

XML keeps data stored separately from the format in which it is displayed. What applies the format to the data is the style sheet you use. Cascading style sheets (CSS) and XSL (Extensible Style Language) are two common methods of applying formatting to an XML document. Because the style sheet and the data are housed separately, you can switch style sheets according to your project objectives and audience and never have to recode or reformat the data.

A Public, International Standard

XML was developed by the World Wide Web Consortium (W3C) with the intention of creating an easy-to-use, easy-to-read open standard that would allow information exchange across platforms all over the world. The W3C is a public organization with the sole purpose of creating standards and new technologies for the Internet. You can find out more about the W3C and its various activities (including in-depth information on the development and application of XML for businesses and individuals) by going to *www.w3.org*.

Note   What is an *open standard*? A technology based on an open standard is open for use and development by the public; there are no licensing fees or proprietary standards owned by a specific company or organization.

Reusable Data

When you separate form from function in this way, it's a simple thing to put the function in another form. In other words, because XML data is stored independently of the form in which it's displayed, you can easily fit it into other formats. XML data that started out as part of a college textbook, for example, could be reused as a series of Web articles, a brochure, a syllabus, a Microsoft PowerPoint presentation, or a blurb in a bookstore catalog.

Wholesale catalogs for specific audiences can be generated on the fly if you've used XML as your data-storage standard. Suppose, for example, that your business sells computer equipment. In the past, you've sent out full-size catalogs (which is a costly endeavor and often provides a low rate of return). If all your catalog data is saved in XML format, you can query the database for a subset of clients (perhaps all customers who purchased equipment from you 24 months previously, customers who bought PCs, customers who bought laptops, and so on) and produce a targeted catalog specifically for that subgroup of all customers on your list. Similarly, you can use this same approach to develop customized solutions for specific clients, departments, industries, and more. The data is the valuable entity, and with XML, you can use that data smarter and more efficiently, and give it a farther reach than it has ever had before.

XSLT (Extensible Stylesheet Language for Transformations) allows you to transform documents into a new form. This is especially important for bringing legacy data into an XML format and transforming it to fit your XML standards.

Write Your Own Schema

Although XML was supported in a limited fashion in Microsoft Word version 2002 (you could save Word documents as XML files), there was no flexibility in terms of the schema used (you had to use Word's built-in schema) or the creation of industry or business-specific applications.

The XML support in Office 2003 gives users the option of attaching customized XSDs (XML Schema Definitions). You can choose to save your documents in Word's default schema (WordML) and attach your own customized (called *arbitrary*) schema that describes the language and functionality you need in your business everyday.

> **Note** The development of custom XML schemas for business applications—as well as the creation and enhancement of XML applications using tools such as smart documents, smart tags, and InfoPath technology—provide a huge opportunity for solutions developers. We are just now beginning to see how XML can streamline the use of data and communications in business, and solutions developers will be key in expanding our understanding of what's possible and providing the means to fully apply the power of XML in our daily tasks.

XML: A Common Denominator

Because XML stores data independently of the format used to display the data, it provides a common denominator for information storage and exchange. Businesses that are equipped to work with XML have a key to unlocking the supply of out-of-reach data stored in antiquated systems and software formats. If they can convert the data to XML, they can put the data to use in any number of other applications and resources.

XML is supported in the new versions of Word, Excel, and Access in an unprecedented way. Although Microsoft Excel version 2002 previously offered some support for XML, and Word 2002 users were able to save their files in XML format if they wanted to, the level of XML support now built into Office 2003 enables users to do all kinds of tasks previously unavailable in the program:

- **Use XML for data analysis.** In Excel you can use the XML features to work with structured, tabular data for calculations and analyses.

- **Author, edit, and manage content.** You can use the XML features in Word to work with large areas of text or mixed content, creating flexible layouts and formatting with XML markup.

- **Store and report on data.** The XML features in Access enable you to store data in relational database tables and create reports based on that data. You can also use Access to transform files from other formats into XML and Access-supported forms.

- **Gather information.**   Not only can you create documents based on XML that prompt users for specific input, you can also use the new Microsoft Office InfoPath 2003 technology to put XML to work in highly structured, dynamic forms for data gathering.

XML for Businesses

If you've been concerned about the long-term data-management considerations your business is facing, you already grasp the benefit of having an open international standard for data exchange. XML gives you a simple, usable form in which to store your data—one that will be around as long as you are. Your data can be ported into various applications and platforms, and will eventually be used in ways we haven't even thought of yet. With the help of solutions developers, the continuing work of the W3C, and the increasing adoption and integration of XML support in major worldwide applications like Office 2003, XML will rapidly become the common denominator for business data exchange—interdepartmentally as well as across industries and nations, and around the world.

Here are a few of the specific ways XML can help businesses work smarter and more efficiently:

- XML data enables businesses to save data once and use it many times, in a virtually unlimited number of applications.

- XML is flexible so that solutions developers can create specific schema and applications based on the needs of individual businesses and industries.

- XML is an open international standard, enabling businesses to develop data-management applications with off-the-shelf tools and avoid costly licensing fees.

- XML enables businesses to access and use legacy data and safeguard today's data for future use.

- Familiar interfaces (such as Word 2003, Excel 2003, and Access 2003) make it easy for end users to work with XML applications without retraining.

XML for Developers

The far-reaching support of XML in Office 2003 is a major opportunity for solutions developers interested in developing schema as well as specific add-on applications to help businesses take the best advantage of XML technology. Here are a few ways solutions developers can take advantage of the XML support built into Office 2003:

■ Create powerful XML templates and solutions using Office 2003 tools (Smart documents, InfoPath templates, and smart tags).

■ Design and offer customized schema and transforms for applications-specific tasks, such as creating corporate profile reports, news articles, resumes, personnel reviews, and more.

■ Create solutions for content repurposing and Web publishing in a variety of forms.

■ Design dynamic forms that gather information for businesses and save to a database with a single click.

■ Develop tools for transferring information from legacy systems and forms into XML-supported systems.

■ Design user helps and in-document prompts (via smart tags) to facilitate data-entry and custom publishing options.

From the Experts

Frank Rice, of the MSDN Office Developer Center (*msdn.microsoft.com/office*), says that the XML support in Office 2003 makes things much easier on developers. "Development time (with XML) is very rapid compared to writing VBA code; *extensible* means you can change it or add to it. Let's say your client company comes and says, 'We've added different fields, we've gotta do *this*, we're interested in *this*....' Instead of having to redo all the VBA code, you can say "OK, we'll just redo this element, add this, pull this one over...." Twenty minutes later, you're done. Additionally, says Rice, XML solutions are easy to deploy. "You just put templates up on a server. XML is all text; no proprietary format is used, so you don't have to be a rocket scientist to figure it out."

XML Support in Office 2003

Although the XML support features that are new throughout Office add exciting new custom development possibilities for developers and IT professionals, the actual day-to-day work with XML has been designed with the everyday information worker in mind. Users in Word, Excel, and Access don't have to be familiar with XML to use the XML features; in fact, they don't have to know anything about XML at all. With a few simple procedures, users can attach XML schema, add XML tags in documents, or create an Excel grid and fill it with XML data simply and easily.

Word 2003 XML Features

Key XML features in Word 2003 focus on allowing users to view, work with, and save XML files easily. Users can create and attach their own custom schemas that can work alongside Word XML or be used alone. XSL transforms save the document in different forms for different views and are available whenever a Word file is opened or saved. Automatic validation makes sure the tags users enter are correct according to the attached schema, and the ability to query a database and import XML data to a Word document ensures that information is as current as possible in reports, proposals, and more. All these possibilities and others make working with XML in Word a simple but powerful feature for changing the way data is prepared, used, shared, and saved for the future.

From the Experts

Michael J. Young, author of *Microsoft Office Professional Edition 2003 Inside Out* and *XML Step by Step* (Microsoft Press) sees the capability of using custom XML schemas and working within the familiar interface to be Word's two strongest XML points. Now for the first time, for example, you can save your book data in an inventory database by using the familiar Word interface. It simply involves writing a new XML schema or attaching an existing one to a Word document and then using Word as a general-purpose document with XML. This means end users can work seamlessly in Word to capture valuable information as part of their familiar tasks.

The XML Task Pane

XML now has its own task pane in Word, first giving you the means to attach an XML schema (you actually do this by using the Templates and Add-Ins dialog box, available through the Tools menu); then showing the tree structure of your XML document so that you can navigate easily through the document. By using the features in this task pane, you can easily add XML tags into your document while you work. (See Figure 5-1.) Word checks tags against the applied schema to make sure that the code is well formed.

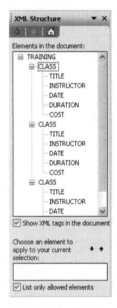

Figure 5-1   The task pane displays the tree structure of the current XML document and enables you to click and add tags while you work.

Working in Tag View

One of the major enhancements in Word is the addition of XML tag view. When you open an XML document and begin to work, any tags you add (or tags that are already present) appear as a kind of graphical bracket around the word, phrase, paragraph, or entire document. Figure 5-2 shows a document in tag view.

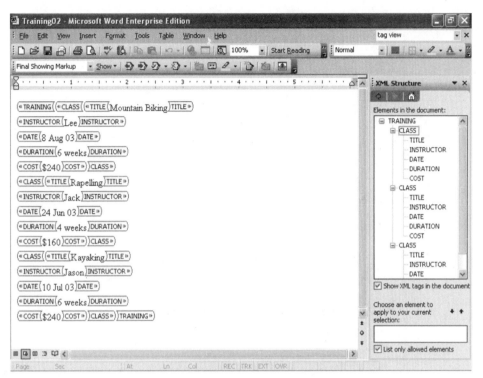

Figure 5-2   Tag view enables you to see at a glance where the XML tags are in your document and how they are nested.

> **Tip**   You can turn tag view off and on by clicking the Show XML tags in the document check box in the task pane.

Attaching a Schema

Word now makes the process of adding a schema simple as well. Choose Tools, Templates And Add-Ins, and click the XML Schema to see the various ways you can work with XML schema in your document. (See Figure 5-3, on the next page.)

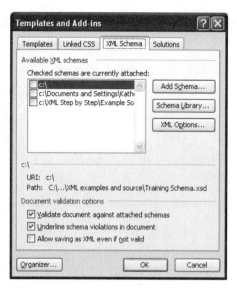

Figure 5-3 You can select and add a schema to your current document in the XML Schema tab of the Templates and Add-Ins dialog box.

Tip You can add more than one schema to a single document if you like. Word will apply both sets of definitions and rules and alert you if there is a conflict.

After you attach a schema and click OK, Word evaluates the incoming schema to see whether it's properly formed. If there are errors in the code, Word will alert you and stop the attachment until the code is corrected.

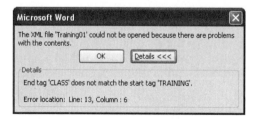

XML Open and Save Features

When you open an XML file in Word and choose XML files from the Files Of Type list in the Open dialog box, you also have the option of applying an XSL transform as you open the file. Display the context menu by clicking the small arrow to the right of the Open button to find the Open With Transform option.

> **Note** An XSL transform allows you to display an XML document in different views; for example, perhaps you are opening a report file that you want to display on the Web. Applying a transform allows you to see the file in a Web-based format without making modifications to the file itself.

When you choose XML Document in the Save As type field of the Save As dialog box (see Figure 5-4), two XML-specific options appear to the left of the Save button. You can click the Apply Transform check box to enable the Transform button; then click that button to choose the transform you want to apply.

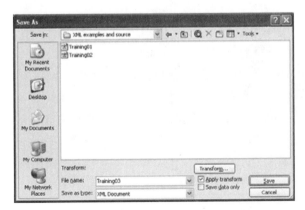

Figure 5-4 Word makes it easy to save the XML file in different formats.

> **Note** Users can manually attach an XML Schema Definition (XSD) file or apply an Extensible Stylesheet Language Transformation (XSLT) to an existing XML file, but Word adds another convenience to simplify this process. Word remembers associated files and gives the user the option of attaching the appropriate XSD or XSLT when a file that matches a recognized category is opened.

Excel 2003 XML Features

Excel's XML features have been significantly expanded over the capabilities in Excel 2002. In that version, XML was first introduced through the application of the XML Spreadsheet Schema (XMLSS); but now users can apply their own schemas and use Excel to import, work with, and export XML data. In addition to this big enhancement, XML features in Excel provide the following:

- Opening, working with, and saving XML files without the need for transforms

- Separation of data from display

- Creating queries to retrieve information stored in a database; allowing for up-to-the-minute data analysis and reporting

- Faster, easier XML support

- A visual mapping tool that enables developers to create structures without writing any code

- A Lists feature that assists users in creating and modifying data lists

- Easy import and export of XML data

- Built-in support for easy data exchange with SharePoint Team Services

The sections that follow take a closer look at the key XML features available in Excel 2003.

Figure 5-5 displays the XML Structure task pane available in Excel. When you first display the task pane, Excel asks whether you want to find a structured (XML) document, create a new one, or add structure to this document (which means adding a schema to your current data file). When you click Create New in the XML Structure task pane, Excel switches to XML design mode and prompts you to select a schema.

Figure 5-5   The XML Structure task pane in Excel enables you to map XML elements to your worksheet and customize the design.

Importing and Exporting XML Data

Importing an XML file is as simple as clicking the Import button on the XML toolbar. The XML toolbar is a new addition in Excel 2003, providing quick and easy access to import, export, and refresh actions.

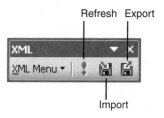

When you click Import, the Import XML dialog box appears so that you can choose your file. Excel asks you to choose the range for the imported data and then places the information in list form in the range you specified. (See Figure 5-6.)

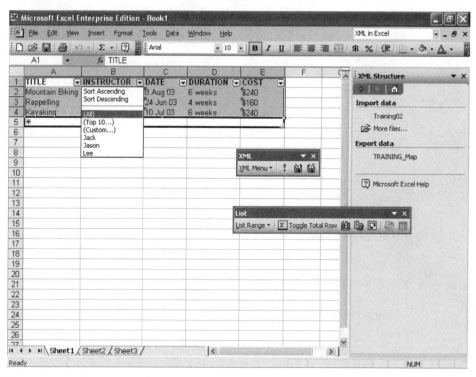

Figure 5-6   The imported XML data is placed in a data list in the specified range.

Excel prompts you if there's a problem with your imported data by displaying a small flag on problem cells. When you click the cell, an exclamation point icon appears. Click that icon, and a submenu appears, letting you know what the problem is and listing possible corrective actions. (See Figure 5-7.) This helps even new XML users understand how to save more accurate and usable data.

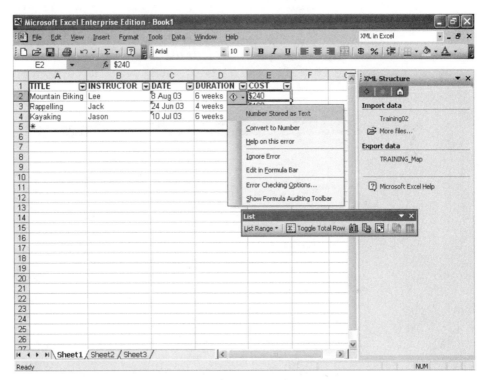

Figure 5-7   Excel lets you know if there's a problem with the imported data.

> **More Info** The Lists feature gives you additional, easy-to-use tools for organizing, viewing, analyzing, and sharing data in your Excel worksheets. For more on Excel's List feature, see Chapter 8, "Microsoft Office 2003 Productivity Enhancements."

Exporting XML data in Excel is as simple as selecting the data you want to export, clicking the Export button in the XML toolbar, and choosing a folder and filename for the file. The file is exported in straight XML format, ready to be incorporated in other XML applications.

```
Class_list - Notepad
File  Edit  Format  View  Help
<?xml version="1.0" encoding="UTF-8" standalone="yes"?>
<TRAINING>
        <CLASS>
                <TITLE>Mountain Biking</TITLE>
                <INSTRUCTOR>Lee</INSTRUCTOR>
                <DATE>8 Aug 03</DATE>
                <DURATION>6 weeks</DURATION>
                <COST>$240</COST>
        </CLASS>
        <CLASS>
                <TITLE>Rappelling</TITLE>
                <INSTRUCTOR>Jack</INSTRUCTOR>
                <DATE>24 Jun 03</DATE>
                <DURATION>4 weeks</DURATION>
                <COST>$160</COST>
        </CLASS>
        <CLASS>
                <TITLE>Kayaking</TITLE>
                <INSTRUCTOR>Jason</INSTRUCTOR>
                <DATE>10 Jul 03</DATE>
                <DURATION>6 weeks</DURATION>
                <COST>$240</COST>
        </CLASS>
</TRAINING>
```

Mapping XML Data

The new visual mapping tool in Excel allows you to add XML elements to your workbooks by dragging and dropping them onto the current worksheet. Figure 5-8, shows the map that is created from a sample XML schema. The XML structure is shown in a tree-like form. You can use parts of the structure by dragging branches or individual items (or the entire list) to your worksheet.

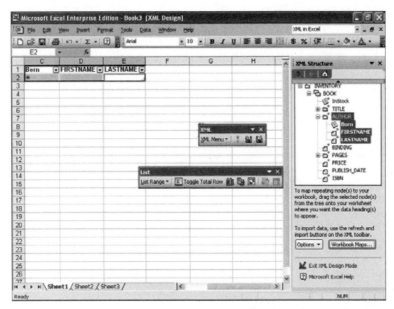

Figure 5-8   The visual mapping tool enables you to create XML worksheets by dragging and dropping XML elements.

Tip   You can add additional workbook maps to the current document by clicking the Workbook Maps button in the XML Structure task pane and clicking Add.

Access 2003 XML Features

The XML changes in Access include fewer end-user features than Excel and Word but expand the flexibility and functionality of Access. Now you can import an XML file (and information from SharePoint Team Services, which also comes in as XML) directly into your Access data tables. Additionally, you can export Access data as straight XML, giving you the means to produce data from a variety of formats in XML output.

From the Experts

Frank Rice, from the MSDN Office Developer Center (*msdn.microsoft.com/office*), thinks the biggest benefit in the XML support in Access 2003 is that it "allows you to transform an XML form coming in and an XML form going out. If you've got an Adobe file and you're translating with an XSL that Access can recognize, when you save it out, you can use a transformer to transform it back. No data maps are needed. Access will take a straight XML file and produce a raw XML file as output. This means you can take a file in another application (such as Lotus Notes), and a good developer can come up with a transform file for it. So instead of the two formats being totally incompatible, we can take this file, run the XSL file to transform the data, and then read it into Access. You can do the same thing going out."

Importing XML Data

There are a number of import options when you bring XML data into Access. A new Import XML dialog box includes an Options button you can click to display the various types of imports available. (See Figure 5-9.) These choices enable you to import only the structure of the XML file, import both structure and data, or append the XML data to an existing Access table.

Figure 5-9   The Import XML dialog box in Access enables you to choose whether to import the structure or both the structure and data, or simply append data to an existing table.

After you click OK, Access imports the data and displays a completion message. The new XML data is placed in a table in your current database. You can open and work with the table as normal.

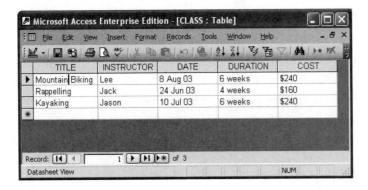

Exporting XML Data

When you export a table as XML data in Access 2003, you've got a number of options to use to control the type of output produced. Begin the export by right-clicking the table in the Database window; then choose XML in the Files of type list. The Export XML dialog box enables you to choose whether you want to export data only, the schema only, or the presentation of the data.

If you want to further control the output, you can click More Options to display additional choices for the output of the XML, XSD, and XSL files.

> **Tip** When you export forms and reports, Access generates the output file using an XML-based language called ReportML. When you generate tables, queries, and datasheets, the output resembles a spreadsheet.

Summary

This chapter has provided a first look at the far-reaching XML support features incorporated into Office 2003. The integration of XML makes Office 2003 more flexible, more powerful, and more adaptable to enterprise-wise applications than ever before. Although this chapter has spotlighted a number of the key XML additions in Word, Excel, and Access, you'll get a much better feel for the seamless application and easy functionality of XML in Office 2003 when you try it for yourself. Whether you're an end user, a decision-maker, or a developer, you'll want to learn more about this highly flexible and widely accepted new standard for data exchange, publication, and storage.

6

XML Applied: Smart Documents, Smart Tags, and Microsoft Office InfoPath 2003

Support for XML in Microsoft Office 2003 goes beyond the progressive new features in Microsoft Office Word, Excel, and Access 2003; Office 2003 also includes new and enhanced tools that significantly improve the way organizations make use of their data—on legacy systems as well as in current applications. Chapter 5 provided an overview of XML in Office 2003 and described how the new application-centered features can be of benefit to both businesses and developers. This chapter focuses on three specific areas in which XML support—as well as other improvements—can make a huge difference in the way information workers capture, use, and manage data in their day-to-day tasks. You'll get a first look at smart documents, smart tags, and Microsoft Office InfoPath 2003, and we'll explore both developer and end-user possibilities for each technology.

A Comparison: Smart Documents, Smart Tags, and InfoPath

If you're familiar with these potentially powerful new tools, you might know about the individual features and applications of each one. All of these tools have something in common, beyond their use of XML: opportunities for developers. Each tool provides new areas for developers to explore creating solutions specific to businesses across a wide range of industries. This section gives you a quick comparison to summarize the details you'll be reading about in this chapter.

- **Smart documents** are customized Word or Excel templates created by developers to add information, resources, or functionality to common business operations. A smart document might display in the task pane specific format-related information, links to additional resources, or information about routing the document to the next person in an approval process.

- **Smart tags** are context-sensitive tags that appear when a particular data item is recognized in the text, offering workers a menu of options related to their current task. Smart tags enable information workers to do additional research, fill in text with data retrieved from a database, apply a special format, or perform any number of customized actions designed by solutions developers.

- **InfoPath** is an all-new technology that mixes dynamic form-creation with text-editing features in the familiar Office interface. InfoPath enables businesses to capture—in industry-standard XML format— bits of information that are often hard to gather and apply in a useful way; data from status reports, meeting agendas, memos, financial projections, and more. InfoPath includes two views—one for filling in a form and another for designing a form. Opportunities exist for developers in creating customized XML schemas for specific industries and in designing methods for incorporating current forms into InfoPath.

Smart Documents

At first glance, the concept of smart documents seems pretty simple. A smart document would anticipate what you're creating, know what you need, and offer the resources to help you create it. It might offer you certain equations for particular financial procedures or suggest a disclaimer paragraph for the end of the proposal you're writing. A smart document would save recognized data in familiar ways, keep track of your personal user settings, and be able to provide additional data or prompts when you need them.

Smart Documents: Quick Facts

Here are some quick facts about smart documents and the way they're distinguished from smart tags and InfoPath:

■ Smart documents work with Word and Excel.

■ Developers create smart documents solutions for end users.

■ Smart documents display customized helps (prompts, links, actions, and more) in a Document Actions task pane.

■ Smart documents are context-sensitive and interactive in the sense that they respond to users' actions in a document.

■ Smart documents use XML schemas to provide the structure of the created document.

■ Deployment of smart documents is simple; Word or Excel templates can be placed on a server or even sent as an attachment to an e-mail message.

The idea behind smart documents is exactly that: documents that enable you—as an IT manager, developer, or expert end user—to build business-specific information into the Word or Excel documents your end users work with. Smart documents might help users in the following ways:

■ **Providing help with formatting.** For documents with specific formatting instructions (for example, a style sheet used by an online magazine to enable writers to HTML-code their writing), a smart document can provide formatting hints and helps as well as lend tagging capability and access to a tag library. Writers could simply click a tag to insert it or search for help to determine which tags to use by clicking a link that takes them to an HTML reference.

■ **Prompting users to add information.** Some documents and spreadsheets include boilerplate text or common features that a smart document can add automatically. For example, suppose that a legal disclaimer is added at the bottom of every product description of a new prescription drug offered by a pharmaceutical company. A smart document can prompt the user to add the boilerplate text and give him or her the option of adding a disclaimer that has been written in different ways for different audiences.

■ **Automating a process.** Smart documents can actually "know" when they are complete and route themselves to the next person in the approval process of a business proposal. When the next person reviews the document, he or she can click programmed Accept or Reject buttons to send the document along to be printed and then added to a document library, perhaps on a Microsoft SharePoint Team Services site.

> **Note** These are just a few ideas for possible application of smart documents. Because this technology offers a wide open opportunity for developers, it will be interesting to see how their creative minds make the most of these powerful and flexible features to help end users working in the familiar Word and Excel interfaces.

Smart Document Possibilities

Smart documents provide a great opportunity for developers to create custom smart document applications for businesses. In a doctor's office, for example, smart documents might enable office personnel to do the following:

■ Create a referral letter to a particular specialist using boilerplate information suggested by the smart document

■ Automatically route reports to various doctors in the practice

■ Track, store, and update information related to consultations

■ Easily look up information on treatment plans, prescriptions, health insurance, and more

■ Provide prompts related to a specific patient, such as the date of the last visit, the attending doctor, and so on

In a car dealership, smart documents could take care of these tasks:

■ Control vehicle customization worksheets that track costs of specific custom items and apply them to pricing per unit

■ Provide customer service workers with links to information about a specific customer's car and service record

■ Insert boilerplate legal information for lease and purchase contracts

- Allow workers to create, save, fax, or e-mail customer-satisfaction surveys

- Generate a chart based on car sales for a specific time period and inserting the chart in a Word report

  In a Web design firm, smart documents could provide these services:

- Format conventions and templates for project proposals for different types of clients

- Create status reports with prompts and approvals for the various stages of the Web design project

- Link to the picture library associated with an individual project

- Prompt for text describing specific Web-design tasks (for inclusion as boilerplate text in client proposals)

- Automatically post of critical documents to a SharePoint Team Services site so that remote members can check project status and download important files

Smart Documents for End Users

What will an information worker see when he or she works with a smart document? In some cases, the experience might be completely transparent. With the familiarity of Word and Excel task panes, users are now accustomed to looking for help with tasks and procedures by going to the panel along the right side of the work window. Because a smart document provides a custom-ized, document-specific task pane, users might not actually realize they are working with smart-document technology.

The smart document is aware of the cursor position and can display information in the task pane related to the worker's specific task or action. The information might take any number of forms, including these:

- Displaying a listing of product names and numbers when the user enters information in a specific field

- Providing links to information related to the user's current task

- Prompting the user with the next step in a process

- Giving suggestions for content or actions

A user might receive the smart document via e-mail or by downloading it from the Web. When he or she opens the file, Office 2003 does the necessary security checks to ensure that the document was sent by a trusted provider. If the security measures check out and the user approves the installation, the template is installed on the user's local machine, along with the supporting files needed to provide the smart document content.

Smart Documents for Developers

The smart document itself is a combination of more than one technology. Developers can use XML schemas to set up the structure of a Word or Excel document and create a custom DLL using Microsoft Visual Basic 6.0, Visual Basic .Net, C++, and C#. The smart documents allow developers to use XML structures to connect their documents to databases and build actions and logic into a document information workers use every day. This makes data more accessible across organizations; provides significant, relevant help for end users; reduces duplication of effort; and lessens the error margin in data entry and manipulation. Moreover, because smart documents can update automatically from trusted servers, developers can work at the server level instead of deploying to individual user systems.

> **Tip**   A *dynamic-link library* (DLL) is a file (with a .dll extension, naturally) that contains a library of common functions used by applications. This library is dynamically linked to the application.

Enhanced Smart Tags

Smart tags were first introduced in Microsoft Office XP, offering end users context-sensitive tags that provided a submenu of options based on what they were trying to do. That introduction of smart tags was able to recognize dates, times, and places, as well as contact names, addresses, and phone numbers. The technology provided developers with the means to create custom smart tag solutions, and in the time since that release, a number of interesting and effective smart tags have been made available to businesses in a variety of industries.

> **Tip**   To see some of the smart tags that were developed for the first incarnation of smart tag technology, visit Office eServices on the Web at *http://office.microsoft.com/services/*.

Smart Tags for Businesses

How will businesses use smart tags? In terms of corporate possibilities, companies who want their employees to be able to link to critical internal resources will use smart tags. Smart tags will be ideal for process documents such as invoices or expense reports. For example, suppose that a user is entering a tracking number. A smart tag recognizes the item, and when the user clicks the smart tag, the menu offers the user the ability to view—directly from the current document—that particular order in the inventory system. Another option on the smart tag menu might fill in the details from that invoice automatically, saving the user keystrokes, time, and error-checking.

Smart Tags: Quick Facts

Here are some quick facts about the changes in Smart Tags for Office 2003:

- Smart tags have been extended to new Office applications and are now available in Microsoft Office PowerPoint 2003 and Access.

- Developers can use XML to create and modify smart tags.

- Smart tags can now automatically carry out an action as soon as a specific tag is recognized.

- Developers have more control over hiding, displaying, or changing the look of customized smart tags.

- Developers can create customizable smart tags that enable property changes.

Users already understand the functionality of smart tags. In Office XP, smart tags offered special formatting options (such as Paste Special) as well as certain recognizers such as contact names, dates, and times. Smart tags, especially used in conjunction with smart documents, have the power to merge disparate corporate processes into more efficient sharing of information. The easy exchange of XML data among applications and databases—or to lists on a SharePoint Team Services site—enable businesses to make critical data available to trusted sources in a variety of integrated ways.

> **Tip** The smart tag application programming interface (API) library has been expanded to include new resources for developers. The smart tag library is named Microsoft Smart Tags 2.0 Type Library, and you can watch for it on *www.msdn.microsoft.com/downloads*. To learn more about planning, implementing, and deploying enterprise smart tags, you can download and read the Smart Tag Enterprise Resource Kit from the same site.

What's New with Smart Tags in Office 2003?

Smart tags now do more and are more flexible than ever before. Developers will find they have more control over the smart tags they create and will be able to develop and deploy smart tags easily. XML support throughout Office 2003 adds an additional boost by enabling developers to use XML to extend MOSTL, the smart tag recognizer and action handler, without going back into the code. Specifically, smart tags in Office 2003 have been enhanced in the following ways:

- Improved support for smart tags in Word, Excel, and Outlook.

- New support for smart tags in PowerPoint and Access.

- Recognition of regular expression and context-free grammar.

- New smart tag properties allow developers to create customizable smart tags.

- Smart tag actions can run directly when a recognizer identifies a string as a smart tag.

- Cascading menus give developers the option of providing users with additional choices.

- Deployment for all users on a machine instead of only the person who installed them.

- Developers can enable or disable the smart tag button and underline for specific smart tags by controlling tag properties.

- Developers can create temporary smart tags with limited functionality.

- Smart tags can also be assigned a time limit so that they expire automatically.

The sections that follow introduce you to some of the key features of Office 2003 smart tags.

From the Experts

Frank Rice, of the Microsoft Office Developers Network (*www.msdn.microsoft.com/office*), explains developing smart tags with XML as compared to creating a DLL: "Smart tags can be created from either an XML file or by using a DLL. The XML approach is ideal for developers who want to develop and deploy smart tags quickly. The DLL approach is more complicated but gives the developer a great deal more flexibility than the XML approach."

New Applications for Smart Tags
In Office XP, smart tags were available in a fairly limited fashion in Word, Excel, and Outlook. Now, in Office 2003, the smart tag functionality in Word and Excel has been improved so that all smart tags in both applications work together more gracefully. Smart tags have been added to PowerPoint and Access as well. In PowerPoint, a smart tag might be used to provide product details about a particular cell phone model or to offer additional information about a new HR evaluation program or benefits package.

Free Expression and Context-Free Grammar
Free expression for a smart tag is more than freedom of speech—it's the flexibility to enable smart tags to recognize a variety of phrases and terms, even when users don't enter them exactly according to expectations. The addition of XML to MOSTL (the Microsoft Office Smart Tag Lists mentioned earlier) enables

you, for example, to create a smart tag that recognizes a wide range of dates in multiple forms or understands the many ways end users might enter a company or product name.

Smart Tag Actions

You can add smart tag actions that are executed automatically when an entry is recognized. This type of smart tag might be used, for example, to display links to product information when the product name is entered in the document. Smart tags can also automatically apply formats to specific phrases, insert additional text, and perform any number of customized tasks.

Customizable Smart Tags

Developers can allow users to set properties for individual smart tag recognizers in Office 2003. Now users can click the Properties button of a customizable smart tag to choose specific options. For example, a user might want to change the smart tag color for a particular type of smart tag, or select a different action (such as filling a field automatically) instead of the default action. Figure 6-1 shows the Properties button users can click to customize available smart tags.

Figure 6-1   The Smart Tags tab in the AutoCorrect dialog box provides a Properties button users can click to change the properties of some smart tags.

> **Tip**   A *recognizer* is the term for the specific item in an Office 2003 application that triggers a smart tag; it's the phrase or term the smart tag recognizes. Types of recognizers include dates, times, phone numbers, people's names, and financial symbols.

Cascading Menus

Developers can now easily create cascading menus for smart tags that give end users additional information and options. This allows developers to group related menu items and increase the functionality of menus. Figure 6-2 shows a cascading smart tag menu.

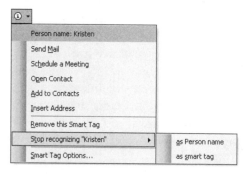

Figure 6-2   Smart tag menus can now cascade in Office 2003.

Temporary Smart Tags

Temporary smart tags function only when the document is open and are not saved with the document, so business-critical information is not saved with the file. You might use this, for example, to display information related to vendor bids when the purchasing manager is viewing the file, but after he approves and signs off on the file, the tags are automatically disabled and others viewing the file do not have the same access to vendor information.

Introduction to InfoPath

Finally in this chapter we come to the *coup de grace* of XML-specific offerings: Microsoft Office InfoPath 2003. This exciting, new XML-based technology offers organizations a way to use dynamic forms with rich editing features to gather important information that is often scattered throughout their business processes. The data, which is captured in XML form, can immediately be put to work throughout an organization and used in a variety of forms.

From the Experts

Acey Bunch, author of *Introducing Microsoft Office InfoPath 2003* (Microsoft Press, 2003), describes the process of using InfoPath: "You design a form, deploy it to your users, and as they use it and save the info, it is saved into a standardized XML format." This is a huge benefit for businesses working with many data-entry applications and provides native support for XML Web services. "Anybody who wants to merge forms or work with data aggregation" will benefit from using InfoPath. "We're using it now on my team. Every week we send the manager the status report; all on SharePoint. I click the form and fill it in. At the end of the week, she gets this merged, nicely formatted form with data. Nicely done with clicks...no code...it's all XML."

Because XML is the native file format for InfoPath, data gathered in InfoPath forms can be shared easily and efficiently. InfoPath works with any customer-defined schema, which means that developers can design customized schema to solve any number of data-gathering needs. And because XML stores data in a highly structured, yet highly flexible, format organizations can ensure that their critical data is standardized across applications.

InfoPath will help transform organizations that rely heavily on forms—paper or electronic—to gather data pertinent to key business processes. InfoPath helps integrate business processes with an intuitive interface (that resembles the best of the other Office applications) and a dynamic method of collecting information. Because InfoPath puts XML in the hands of everyday workers—without requiring that they learn to write code or master new procedures—organizations will be able to capture, store, share, and make the best use of their data in an increasingly secure, efficient way.

InfoPath: Quick Facts

Here is a quick list of need-to-know facts about InfoPath:

- XML is InfoPath's native file format.
- Customer-defined schemas can be used with InfoPath.
- InfoPath includes rich text-editing features.
- InfoPath is available on the Tablet PC.
- Sample forms are included with InfoPath you can either use as is or modify to suit your needs.

InfoPath for Businesses

Every business has a method of organizing the information flow from one group to another, one department to another, one level to another. Sales needs to know what Product Development is up to. Marketing needs the latest information on new product specifications. Purchasing stays in close contact with Inventory. Customer Service needs to have direct access to Sales, and managers in each of those areas need information from each of the workers in their departments.

It's staggering to think of the amount of data that already flows through our processes—often not in the most productive ways. The sales manager sitting in a meeting Tuesday afternoon makes a note that inventory is low on a key product; he has to wait until he gets back to his desk to enter that information in a memo, note it in his update report, send an e-mail to his key salespeople who are counting on large orders for that product, and so on. If he were working with InfoPath (and had his Tablet PC with him in the meeting), he could capture that data as "live" information in real time. By noting it on an InfoPath form, he could save it to a database, port it to SharePoint Team Services (where his sales team would see a new announcement about the low stock), or e-mail it directly to those who most need to know.

The primary goal of InfoPath is very simple: to allow businesses to make better use of data by saving information in native XML format, which allows that information to be used in an almost unlimited number of ways, according to the needs of the individual organization. Because InfoPath shares a familiar Office 2003 interface, users will find InfoPath easy and comfortable to learn and use—with little training needed. Developers and form designers will find an intuitive design view that offers forms-based controls as well as rich text-editing features, ensuring that the forms you create for your organization are as effective and accurate as possible.

The Traditional Form Process

Let's follow the path of a traditional status report to see how InfoPath can make a difference in handling process data. Suppose that for a weekly status report, an information worker uses a standard format template in Word and enters the information by typing it in from a paper form she has filled out over the course of the week. She then prints a copy of the report and places it in her supervisor's inbox. Or, alternatively, she e-mails a copy of the report to the supervisor. All the information is there on the screen, but it is simple text—not live information that can be applied in any real sense. The supervisor must read, analyze, and perhaps copy and paste the numbers or comments from the report to compile a larger status report that includes similar data from all her staff members. She places each person's information in the appropriate column on her summary report and then prints or e-mails the status report to *her* supervisor. So much effort, and a lot of time invested. But where's the usable data?

Consider this scenario using InfoPath. The status report is now an InfoPath form in which the knowledge worker can type (or write, using a Tablet PC), the data items her supervisor needs to know: How many units shipped this week; how many are outstanding; was this over or under projections; what factors influenced work flow this week; and so on. Some of this information is numerical; other pieces of data are text- or date-based. Because the data gathered is stored in XML format, the underlying schema both controls data entry (making sure numbers are entered in the expected form, for example) and ensures that the information is stored immediately in a back-end database, from which the supervisor (and the supervisor's supervisor) can pull automatic reports when all the reports have been filed.

InfoPath Applications

The last section walked you through one example showing how static information that must be copied and pasted from application to application can be automatically saved and used in InfoPath. Here are some other common business forms that would work well in InfoPath:

- Summary project-planning sheet
- Invoices

- Purchase orders and purchase summaries

- Financial summary report

- Sales analyses

- Travel itineraries

- Memos

- Contact call list

- Timesheets

- Inventory updates

- Employee evaluations

- Expense reports

> **Tip**   InfoPath includes a library of sample forms you can use for your own business processes. You can use the forms as they are or as templates on which to begin building your own custom forms.

Highlights of InfoPath

We've already touched on several of the major benefits of using InfoPath—the native XML format, the easy integration with existing business processes, and the enhanced usability of "live" data captured in a variety of settings. This section details some of the highlights in InfoPath for both end users and form designers.

End users will find that InfoPath provides the following benefits:

- **A familiar Office-like interface.**   The familiar menus—File, Edit, View, Insert, Format, Tools, Table, and Help—enable users to find text-editing features similar to those they know and use in Word. The task pane offers form selection and editing options, similar to other Office applications. (See Figure 6-3, on the next page.)

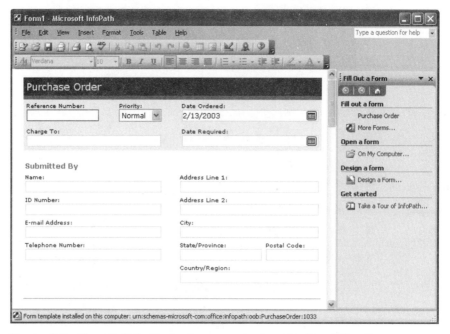

Figure 6-3 The InfoPath Form view appears in a familiar Office-like interface. Users enter information using this view.

- **Requires no special XML coding.** The easy-to-use forms interface enables users to simply click and type (or write) their entries in the form and then save the form as usual. InfoPath does the saving to XML behind the scenes, and because XML is InfoPath's native format, no transforms or exports are needed.

- **Allows easy validation of data entry.** Users who are new to a particular form are sometimes confused about what type of information to enter in a field. Because InfoPath is built on highly structured XML, the attached XML schema will let users know when entered data does not fit the defined form. This helps ensure integrity and consistency of data entered on forms deployed throughout an organization.

- **Rich text-editing features ensure accuracy.** The simple text-editing features of InfoPath enable users to run spell check or use AutoCorrect as they work. This ensures that the entered data is as accurate as possible before submission.

■ **Lets users work at their own pace.** Some form-generating programs insist that users complete the entire form at one sitting; otherwise, the data is lost and the user has to start again later. InfoPath enables the user to stop and save the form at any point and return to it later. The form can be saved on the worker's local hard drive and then submitted to the database (or forwarded along in the approval process) when the form is complete.

For those who will be designing forms in InfoPath, another set of highlights emerges:

■ **Create forms in a WYSIWYG environment.** WYSIWYG, or "what you see is what you get," enables designers to see what they're creating as they're creating it. Design view in InfoPath enables form designers to modify the format of the displayed form and choose to insert controls, display the data source, and manage created views, all without leaving the InfoPath interface. (See Figure 6-4.)

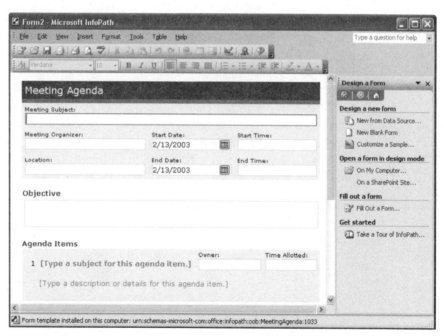

Figure 6-4   Design view in InfoPath gives forms designers tools for working with formats, controls, data sources, and views.

- **Apply layout tables in Design view.** InfoPath makes it easy for form designers to choose the type of layout they want to use by selecting table formats from a pre-designed table layout collection.

- **Use custom-designed schemas.** InfoPath enables designers to create custom forms using a customer-defined schema that defines the type of information being gathered. This enables businesses to determine for themselves what kinds of data they want to collect and how they want to share it throughout the organization.

- **Choose from a library of sample forms.** InfoPath ships with a large library of sample forms that form designers can modify to fit their own business processes. Sample forms include invoices, meeting agendas, travel itineraries, status reports, applicant ratings, performance reviews, and more.

From the Experts

"Microsoft's vision for Office (2003) is to seamlessly connect the information worker to the different islands of data in the enterprise, whether the data is contained in Microsoft Word documents, e-mail messages, an internal company database, or even an external third-party database. To do this, we are altering the paradigm for the Office system of products: instead of asking customers to structure data based on the software product they use to generate that data, we want to enable customers to use the data defined by their own schemas—however they want to structure it." —Jean Paoli, the XML architect behind InfoPath at Microsoft (*www.microsoft.com/presspass/*).

Summary

This chapter has given you a closer look at three key areas in which XML support in Office 2003 is put to good use: smart documents, smart tags, and InfoPath. Smart documents provide a great opportunity for developers to create custom solutions–based templates that are tailored to the needs of information workers in specific industries; smart tags enable businesses and developers to provide workers with pertinent contextual links and actions related to their work in a specific document; and InfoPath digitizes data capture from common business process forms and saves all the information in industry-standard XML. These progressive, exciting additions to Office 2003 allow organizations and individuals to capture data more intentionally, share it more easily, and use it more efficiently, in individual applications, across team projects, or throughout an entire enterprise system.

7

Upgrading, Deploying, and Administering Microsoft Office 2003

Brian Johnson

Whether you're an individual, small-business, or large-enterprise user, the setup and deployment features of Microsoft Office 2003 make it easier than ever to upgrade to the latest version of Office. In this chapter, we'll take a look at a basic upgrade scenario to demonstrate a standalone installation. This single machine upgrade shows you what to expect when moving from Office XP or earlier to Office 2003. Next we'll take a look at tools that administrators can use to make the upgrade to Office as smooth as possible for multiple users. We'll show you tools that make it easy for administrators to maintain Office 2003 installations, and we'll discuss how to keep up with the latest patches and security fixes. Finally we'll discuss the Customer Experience Improvement Program that Microsoft will use to help make Office 2003 a stronger product.

Installing on or Upgrading Office 2003 on a Single Machine

To get started, let's take a look at a typical single-user upgrade to Office 2003. In this case, we'll upgrade a user currently running Office XP on Microsoft Windows XP, but most of what we'll go over in the sections that follow will also apply to users installing Office 2003 for the first time.

You can perform two basic types of upgrades when installing Office 2003. You can upgrade your existing installation of Office, leaving most of your current versions of Office products in place; or you can have the Office 2003 installer remove your current versions of Office products during the install process.

What this means is that you can mix and match the Office products that you have installed on a machine. The number of choices that you have can be a little overwhelming, so unless you know that you're going to completely remove your earlier installation of Office, or that you're going to do a full-on side-by-side install, it's worth taking some time to plan which products you want installed on your machine.

You might be wondering why you should keep or remove any earlier versions of Office products that you currently run. The most important thing to consider is whether Office 2003 changes anything that makes it difficult for you to do your current work. This could include whether macros and add-ins that you now depend on work with Office 2003, whether new features of the product will require time to learn because they work differently from your current version, or even whether the file formats that you use are compatible among different versions of Office products.

> **Note** Side-by-side and custom installations are available for every Office system product except Microsoft Office Outlook 2003. When you install Outlook 2003, you can't keep earlier versions of the product installed.

If you're at all worried about whether the Office 2003 products that you install won't let you accomplish your work, by all means do a side-by-side install so that you have both versions available if you need them. If you're doing mission-critical work in Excel 2002, keep both versions of Excel on your machine and let the installer remove earlier versions of other Office products.

To help you plan your upgrade, write down the versions of the products currently on your machine, along with the names of the Office 2003 products that you want to install, as shown in Figure 7-1. Circle the names of the products you want to keep or install on the machine, and hang onto that list as you run the installer.

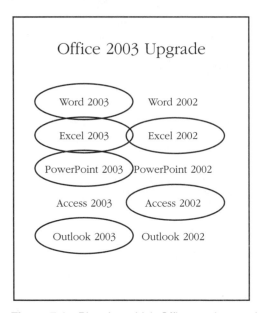

Figure 7-1   Planning which Office products to keep and install.

The Office 2003 Installation Process

Let's take a look at how the installation process will work on a single machine running the default installation configuration. By reviewing this information, you'll be better prepared when it comes time to choose the products and options available in Office 2003, and you'll be aware of the options that you can set if you create a custom administrative install as described later in the chapter.

This scenario assumes you're starting an installation from the Office 2003 CD-ROM or from the default installer from a network share. After you enter your product key and accept the end-user license agreement, you'll see a setup page similar to the one in Figure 7-2, on the next page.

> **Tip**   Make sure your user name and initials are entered properly when you first install Office 2003, because these items are used when you collaborate with others on Office documents.

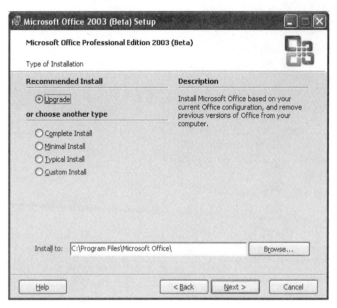

Figure 7-2   Choosing the type of upgrade installation you want to perform.

This is where the branching begins, so you'll need to make some decisions about what you want installed. If you have an earlier version of Office installed on the machine, the default selection is Upgrade. Upgrade will remove your older Office products and replace them with the Office 2003 versions. This is the easiest way to get Office 2003 on your machine, but with that ease you give up some control over what you keep on your machine. The other options include Complete Install, Minimal Install, Typical Install, and Custom Install.

> **Note**   Keep in mind that the Office 2003 installer is a tool that you can use to modify your Office 2003 installation. You can add tools and products later that you omitted during your initial installation. It's much more difficult to reinstall an older Office product once you uninstall it, so take extra care when selecting which legacy products you remove during your Office 2003 installation.

These days, disk space is less of a concern than it has been in the past, but users on laptop computers and those using older hardware sometimes need to keep tabs on how much space a product installation takes. Table 7-1 contains the estimated disk space required for each of the available installation types for Office 2003. Remember that these numbers are only an estimate.

Table 7-1   Disk Space Required for Office 2003

Install Type	Disk Space Required
Complete	458 MB
Minimal	234 MB
Typical	307 MB
Custom	307 MB

You'll notice that the Typical and Custom installation types take the same initial size. This means that the Custom type starts with the same options selected as the Typical installation type, but you have the opportunity to customize what gets installed. The major difference between the Typical installation and the Minimal installation is that Microsoft Office Access 2003 is installed on first use in the Minimal installation rather than with the other products.

Note   Install on first use is an option that adds a feature to the list of what's available to a user, but doesn't actually perform the installation until the user invokes the feature.

The installation type that you choose determines what you see next in the installation process. If you're upgrading, you'll get the Previous Version of Office page like the one in Figure 7-3, on the next page. This page lets you choose which legacy products you want to remove or keep on your machine. You can choose to remove all the previous versions of Office applications, or you can choose only those specific versions that you want to *remove*. Notice the emphasis on remove. If you want to keep a particular product, make sure that the checkbox for that product is *not* checked.

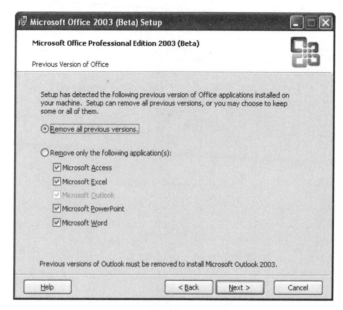

Figure 7-3   Choosing which legacy products to keep or remove.

If you choose the Custom Install path, you're given the opportunity to choose which Office 2003 products you want to install on your machine. If you want to keep your earlier version of Outlook, select the Custom option. Figure 7-4 shows the Custom Setup page. Here you can choose the particular Office 2003 products you want to install.

Tip   If you want to keep running a legacy version of Outlook, clear the Microsoft Outlook box on the Custom Setup page.

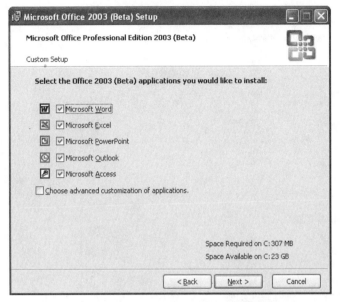

Figure 7-4   Choosing which Office 2003 products you want to install.

The Choose Advanced Customization of Applications checkbox gives you more options for installation, as shown in Figure 7-5, on the next page. You'll use a page much like this one to add and remove features from your Office installation as you need them throughout the life of the product. The Custom Setup page lets you specify which *products* to install, and the Advanced Customization page gives you control over both the products and the product features that get installed. For example, using this page you can choose to install the Speech or Handwriting user input methods.

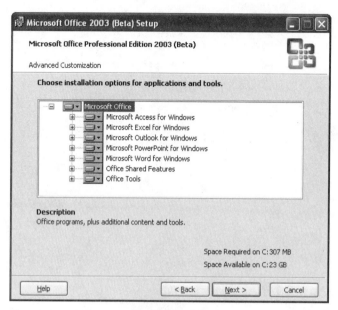

Figure 7-5   The Advanced Customization page lets you specify which features of each product you want to install.

> **Tip**   You can change the type of installation that you want to perform at any time by clicking the Back button.

When you get to the Summary page, you'll see an Install button in place of the Next button in the Setup wizard. This is the point at which your installation will begin. If you chose to remove your legacy Office applications, a utility will run to remove those first. The appropriate Office 2003 files will then be copied locally, and shortcuts will be placed in a Microsoft Office folder item in your All Programs menu.

When your installation completes, you'll see a page like the one shown in Figure 7-6. The page contains two checkboxes that you should consider carefully. The first checkbox is Check The Web For Updates And Additional Downloads. You should check this box if you're connected to the Internet and if you have time to update your machine. The Office page that's opened will give you information about available resources and, more importantly, updates that can help you keep your machine and data secure.

The second option on the Setup Completed page is Delete Installation Files. If you have plenty of drive space, you'll want to keep this checkbox cleared so that any updates to your installation take place locally. This is especially important for laptop users who spend a lot of time off the corporate network. You don't want to be prompted for a CD while you're working away on an airplane at 40,000 feet!

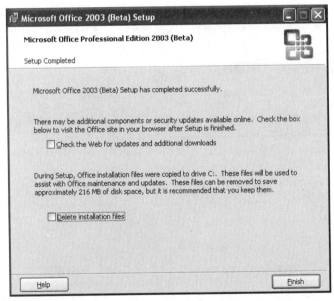

Figure 7-6   The Setup Completed page presents you with post-installation options.

So Which Install Should I Use?

With all these options, you might find yourself confused about what to install. What we've found is that if you do a standard install and keep the installation files on your machine after your install is complete, you'll be prepared for almost anything.

If security is a concern, consider removing features that you don't need or that you don't use. To remove an installed feature, just open Add Or Remove Programs in Control Panel, choose Microsoft Office Professional 2003 (or the version of Office 2003 that you have installed), and click Change. This will reopen the Office Setup Wizard and give you the opportunity to customize your installation. You can always add features back when you need them.

Deploying Office in the Enterprise

One of the best features of Office 2003 is flexibility that it affords to administrators who need to install the product on a number of enterprise machines. Using the tools built into the Microsoft Office 2003 Resource Kit, a network administrator can control the way that Office 2003 is installed on users' workstations. In this section, we'll look at some of the Office Resource Kit tools and demonstrate how the Office 2003 deployment features can make the product rollout as painless and efficient as possible.

The Office Resource Kit

The Microsoft Office 2003 Resource Kit provides tools and guidance for network administrators who need to install Office on enterprise workstations. When Office 2003 ships, you'll be able to download the Office Resource Kit from the Microsoft Web site at *www.microsoft.com/office/ork*. You should also be able to buy a printed version of the kit that includes the software on CD-ROM.

The Microsoft Office 2003 Resource Kit setup program installs a number of tools that you can use to administer and customize Office in the enterprise. The tools we'll talk about right now include the Custom Installation Wizard and the Custom Maintenance Wizard. Table 7-2 contains a complete list of the Office 2003 Resource Kit tools and resources. You'll find the documentation for these tools in the Help file installed by the Resource Kit setup program and at the Office 2003 Resource Kit Web site.

Table 7-2   Tools in the Office 2003 Resource Kit

Item	Description
Answer Wizard Builder	Add your own searchable help content to Office 2003.
Custom Installation Wizard	Deployment tool that makes it easy to create custom Office 2003 installations.
Custom Maintenance Wizard	Tool that helps administrators maintain Office 2003 installations.
Customization Tool Viewers	These viewers let you see the contents of different types of configuration files.
HTML Help Workshop	You can use the Help Workshop to create custom Help that users can access from within Office applications.
Office Policy Templates	ADM (administrative) templates are used with Windows policy tools to control options usually set by the user in the Office 2003 Options dialog box.
Office Converter Pack	Contains file converter utilities.
Outlook Security Form	Tool for administering security features in Office 2003.
Profile Wizard	Tool for creating a user settings file that can be used to set options during Office installation.
Removal Wizard	Tool for removing previous versions of Microsoft Office. You can use this tool after installing Office 2003.

Table 7-3 lists some of the documentation and samples installed with the Office 2003 Resource Kit.

Table 7-3   Office 2003 Resource Kit Samples and Documentation

Item	Description
Customizable Alerts	Customizable Alerts let you create custom error messages for Office 2003.
International Information	Help for using the different language versions of Office 2003 and for using the Multilingual User Interface Packs.
Office Information	Includes specific information about how Office 2003 is installed on workstations.
Package and Definition Files	Package Definition Files (PDFs) are used to deploy Office 2003 using Systems Management Server (SMS).
Book	Includes the electronic documentation for the Office 2003 Resource Kit.

After you install the Office 2003 Resource Kit, you'll find links to all the tools in a new folder in the Microsoft Office Tools folder named Microsoft Office 2003 Resource Kit. The Microsoft Office Tools folder for Office 2003 is now located in the Microsoft Office folder by default.

Creating a Custom Installation

Administrators who want to create a custom installation of Office 2003 will usually generate an installation share that contains the appropriate installation files. Users or administrators will then run the Setup program, a custom link, or a script that will install Office. By customizing some of the configuration files on the installation share, an administrator can control how Office 2003 is installed. Here we'll look at how an administrator might create a simple custom installation.

When creating a custom installation, the first thing that an administrator will do is plan how Office 2003 will be rolled out in the enterprise. This includes some of the same considerations that we discussed for individual users. Are custom applications going to work properly? Are users going to require additional training on new Office 2003 features? Do all the machines meet the minimum requirements for Office 2003? Administrators can find information about planning an Office 2003 deployment in the Resource Kit documentation. We'll assume all those questions have been answered for now so that we can see what goes into building and running the custom deployment.

Using the Office 2003 Custom Installation Wizard

The Custom Installation Wizard is the tool used to modify the Office 2003 installation process. This tool reads the Office 2003 Microsoft Windows Installer (.MSI) file and writes options to a .MST (transforms) file that controls the install options. Administrators can control a large number of options, including the following:

■ Where Office 2003 is installed

■ Whether previous versions of Office are removed

■ Which specific feature sets in Office 2003 are enabled or disabled by default

■ Whether a default application-settings profile is added

■ Whether custom files, shortcuts, and Registry entries are added during installation

■ Which Office security settings are enabled by default

■ How users will customize Microsoft Outlook for the first time

We won't take you through every page of this wizard, but there are a few options of interest to those who are considering whether to customize the installation process for the enterprise.

The first option allows the administrator to specify the product key and automatically accept the end-user license agreement. These options are then cached on the user's machine, making it very convenient to maintain the Office 2003 installation. Figure 7-7, on the next page, shows the Configure Local Caching of Install Source page of the Office 2003 Custom Installation Wizard.

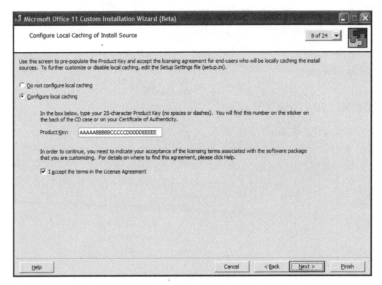

Figure 7-7   Setting up install source-caching options.

A second option of interest lets the administrator determine which versions of older Office products are removed during the installation process. As you can see in Figure 7-8, the administrator can be very specific about which products are removed. This makes it easy to deploy Office 2003 and maintain mission-critical legacy applications on users' machines.

One of the great benefits of this feature is that users don't have to mess with product keys to install the product. This can be helpful in lowering your support costs.

Figure 7-8   Choosing which older versions of a product to keep.

Another important option that administrators are able to set with a custom install configuration is the security level for Office 2003 applications. Office scripting is extremely powerful, and it's an important feature for adding enterprise functionality, but it can be a security problem if the appropriate precautions aren't taken. The Office 2003 Custom Installation Wizard lets you specify the security options important to your network and your company. You can see the Specify Security Level For Outlook dialog box in Figure 7-9.

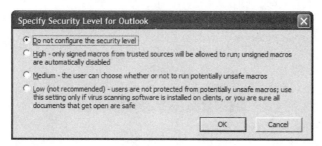

Figure 7-9   Specifying the default security level for the Microsoft Outlook 2003 custom installation.

The Office 2003 Custom Installation Wizard consists of 23 option pages. Most are intuitive, and you can find documentation for the tool and for creating custom installations in the Office 2003 Resource Kit. Figure 7-10 shows the final options page in the Custom Installation Wizard. You can see the other pages in the drop-down list that's open on this page. This list is available from any page in the wizard, and you can use it to jump between the pages you want to customize.

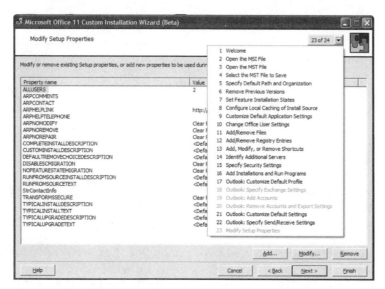

Figure 7-10   Displaying a list of the pages of the Office 2003 Custom Installation Wizard.

When you click Finish, the custom Windows Installer transform file is generated by the wizard, and you're presented with a page that shows you how to use the new transform. To employ the transform, you use the TRANSFORMS option with Setup.exe, specifying the transform as shown in the sample in Figure 7-11. You will also notice that the suggested command line includes some switches that are documented in the Office Resource Kit. The Office 2003 Installer lets you specify a number of installation switches that give you very fine control over how the install process works for users.

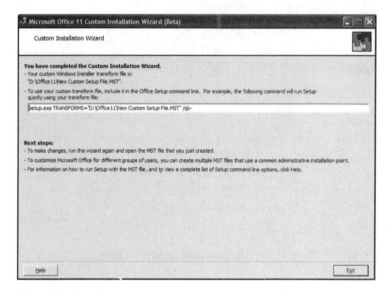

Figure 7-11   The suggested command line for the newly created transform.

As you can tell from this short introduction, the Microsoft Office 2003 Custom Installation Wizard makes it really easy to create a custom installation for Office 2003 and roll it out to your users. In addition to gaining control over the installation process, building a custom install can make life easier for users, allowing them to spend more time working and less time worrying about how to install Office 2003.

> **Tip**   Remember that you can change your transform at any time by reopening it in the Office 2003 Custom Installation Wizard.

Deployment Through Microsoft System Management Server

If your company uses Microsoft System Management Server, you have a number of powerful options for deploying Microsoft Office 2003 in the enterprise. For example, you can use the tools in System Management Server to push a custom Office installation (like the one we created in the last section) to users' desktops. In addition, you can make custom Office installations available through the Add or Remove Programs Control Panel applet, making it easy for users to install Office after rebuilding machines or for administrators setting up machines for new users.

> **Note**   One of the most important capabilities of System Management Server is that it allows administrators to install Office 2003 on machines that don't provide users with administrator privileges. This can help administrators keep the network secure and at the same time make it easy to install applications that would normally require elevated privileges.

Maintaining an Office Installation

Administrators can use the Office 2003 Custom Maintenance Wizard to update these Office 2003 options on machines the product has been installed on:

- Organization name
- Installed features
- User settings
- Custom files and settings
- The administrative install point list
- The Office 2003 security settings
- The default Outlook profile

The Microsoft Office 2003 Custom Maintenance Wizard works by generating or editing a Custom Maintenance Wizard configuration file. This file has a .CMW extension. As you move through the wizard, you'll see options that look similar to the ones we discussed for the Setup wizard and for the Custom Installation wizard. Figure 7-12 shows the Set Feature Installation States page. This page lets you add features to or remove features from the Office 2003 installation. Notice that all options are left unchanged by default.

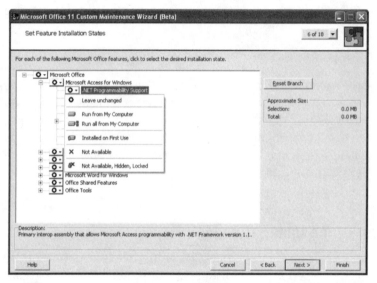

Figure 7-12   Selecting options in the Office 2003 Custom Maintenance Wizard

Once again, an important feature of this wizard is that it lets administrators customize security settings. This makes it easy to change Office 2003 settings throughout the enterprise if security policies change at the company. You can see the Specify Office Security Settings page in Figure 7-13.

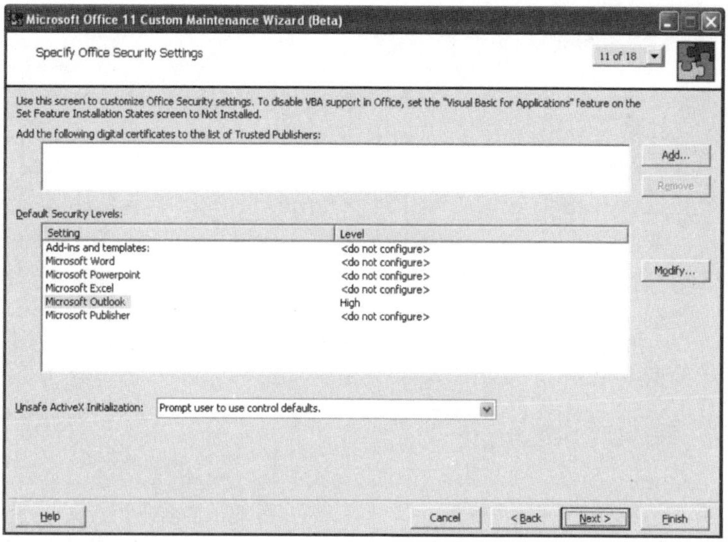

Figure 7-13 Setting security options.

As with the Office 2003 Custom Installation Wizard, the Office 2003 Custom Maintenance Wizard displays a page upon completion that suggests how the new configuration file should be used. This occurs when MaintWiz.exe is called with the name of the .CMW file as one of the options. The default command line for a typical maintenance configuration might look something like this:

```
\ ******************************************************************
MaintWiz.exe /c "d:\My Documents\New Maintenance Data File.CMW" /qb-
 ******************************************************************/
```

The /c option specifies the .CMW used. The /q option specifies quiet mode, meaning the update will be installed without further prompting.

Keeping Office Up to Date

Updates have always been a feature of complex software. In today's networked world, they take on much more importance because many of the fixes shipped by software developers are related to preventing security problems after a product has shipped.

Office 2003 can be updated in a number of ways when the need arises. One method for rolling out fixes is to update the administrative install point for the product and recache and then reinstall the Office 2003 applications on users' computers. You can find information about how to update an administrative install point at the Microsoft Office Resource Kit Web site at the URL listed earlier in the chapter. With this method, the application and the cache are updated, ensuring that changes between the cache and the installed application are the same.

A second way to roll out updates is to perform an administrative update directly on the client machines. As the frequency of patch releases increases, it might be impractical to reinstall Office whenever a patch is released. The administrative updates method involves keeping the Office 2003 installation point at a baseline level and applying updates to the clients only. This helps prevent clients from getting out of sync with the server when updates need to be performed.

In either case, when rolling out Office 2003, you should plan on updates. Administrators should have plans in place for updating enterprise clients when necessary. Doing so can go a long way toward preparation for emergencies, should they arise.

Microsoft Resources

Microsoft Office Professional Edition 2003 Inside Out, by Michael J. Young (Microsoft Press) should be on the shelves soon after the launch of the product. This book can help you plan and execute Office 2003 deployments effectively and painlessly in your enterprise.

In addition, you can get deployment help from a number of Office administration newsgroups. We recommend checking out the following groups on the Microsoft news server:

news://msnews.microsoft.com:/microsoft.public.office.setup
news://msnews.microsoft.com:/microsoft.public.office.officeresourcekit

The Customer Feedback Loop

One of the most important things that customers can do to help improve Microsoft Office is to provide feedback about problems with the product. Microsoft has built into Office 2003 features that make error reporting and feedback easy to provide and quite seamless in the product.

The Service Options dialog box shown in Figure 7-14 is available from the Customer Feedback Options item on the Help menu from the various Office 2003 products. This dialog box lets you choose whether to participate in the Customer Experience Improvement Program. It also provides a link to a Web page for more information about the program.

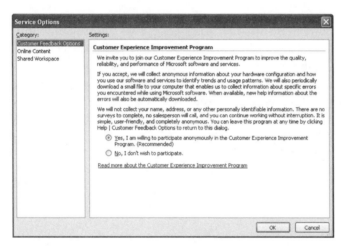

Figure 7-14   Setting Customer Experience Improvement Program preferences.

The Customer Experience Improvement program is a completely anonymous forum that collects information about how you use Microsoft Office 2003 and about the hardware on which you run Office. Microsoft uses this information to improve the various Office 2003 products.

As you can imagine, Microsoft Office 2003 will be installed by millions of users in a fairly short period of time. Microsoft uses the information garnered from the Customer Experience Improvement program to prioritize updates and fixes so that the product becomes stronger over time. One of the positive features of participating in this program is that problems your company has with the product are reported. In essence, your reports to this program become votes for what Microsoft should look at when prioritizing what to update in the product.

> **Tip**   You can change your preference for participating in the Customer Experience Improvement program at any time by toggling your choice in the Service Options dialog box.

Summary

The installation features in Microsoft Office 2003 are designed to make it easy for users to install the product and for administrators to roll the product out to the enterprise. Microsoft Office 2003 Resource Kit tools such as the Microsoft Office 2003 Custom Installation Wizard and the Microsoft Office 2003 Custom Maintenance Wizard help administrators create and maintain Office 2003 deployments that are painless and easy on the user. Keep in mind that automated feedback to Microsoft can help improve everyone's Office 2003 experience. Consider participating in the Customer Experience Improvement Program to help put your Office 2003 issues on Microsoft's radar.

8

Microsoft Office 2003 Productivity Enhancements

Up to this point in the book, we've focused on the new features, tools, and technologies in Microsoft Office 2003. But this release includes more than great new features—it also offers many productivity enhancements in each of the core applications, as well as additions to Office as a whole. This chapter gives you a quick look at the wide range of improvements that can make your work easier, more productive, more secure, and more flexible.

Office-Wide Enhancements

A number of new and enhanced productivity features are available in various Office 2003 applications. They include improved ways to enter, protect, and share data as well as tools for adding sound, pictures, and scanned data to your current applications.

Using Ink

Most people grumble about their handwriting but still prefer jotting notes on a pad of paper over typing them in Word. What if you could do both? Imagine sitting in a meeting or a coffee shop, scribbling notes on a Tablet PC (or the graphics tablet attached to your desktop computer), and watching your doodles become data.

Ink enhancements in Office 2003 make handwriting a viable option for entering and working with text, numbers, and slides in Microsoft Office Word, Excel, and PowerPoint 2003. Now Tablet PC users can write information and allow the application to transform the data to typed text or preserve the writing as handwriting. The Write Anywhere feature allows you to turn most of your Tablet PC into a writing surface. This means you're not limited to the Input Panel that appears at the bottom of your tablet in portrait mode. You can customize the ink feature by making these changes to Write Anywhere:

■ Adding the Write Anywhere button to the title bar

■ Changing the color and thickness of your writing

■ Modifying the "wait time" between when you write or draw and when the input is displayed

Word automatically converts handwriting to typed text, but you can elect to leave your notes handwritten if you like. To do this, simply enter your text in the Writing Pad of the Input Panel and then click the down-arrow to the right of the Send button. From the displayed list, click Send as Ink. The data is placed in the document at the cursor position, but your handwriting rather than typed text appears.

> **Note** The Send as Ink feature works as a toggle, so Word will continue inputting your handwriting as ink until you choose Send as Text.

Inking Modes

When you use Ink on the Tablet PC, you'll notice three new toolbars:

■ Ink Annotations turns on the annotations feature so that you can add notes on documents, slides, or spreadsheets. A toolbar provides tools for choosing line color and thickness, using an eraser, selecting objects, or stopping annotations.

■ Ink Comments enables the Input Panel or the Write Anywhere feature so that you can add comments directly into the document at the cursor position. A toolbar with only two options—Draw Ink and Erase Ink—appears when you choose Ink Comments.

■ Ink Drawing And Writing displays the Drawing Canvas (and accompanying toolbar) so that you can write or draw a diagram directly into your document. You also can change ink color and thickness and erase ink as needed.

Bubble Comments in Microsoft Office Word 2003

Comment bubbles were a new addition to Word 2002, enabling users to view and respond to comments (in Print Layout and Web Layout views) in bubbles in the right margin of the document. The ink feature in Office 2003 allows you to use Word's bubble comments feature and also provides for handwritten and drawn comments inside the bubbles. This enables you to insert traditional comments using a variety of handwritten, typed, or mixed formats. (See Figure 8-1.)

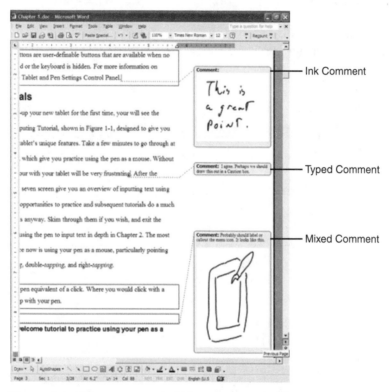

Figure 8-1   You can enter bubble comments in Word with a mix of hand-written, drawn, or typed notes.

> **Tip**   Using comments in this way has advantages over using annotations if several reviewers are commenting on a document. Comments can be tracked, hidden, or organized by reviewer, whereas annotations can be only hidden or displayed.

Cell-Centric Comments in Microsoft Office Excel 2003

In Office 2003, ink annotations you add to your Excel spreadsheets are anchored to the cell that was selected when you created the ink note. This means that no matter how the worksheet might change—cutting and pasting an annotated range from one worksheet to another, inserting or removing columns, and so on—the annotation stays with the cell it is linked to. (See Figure 8-2.)

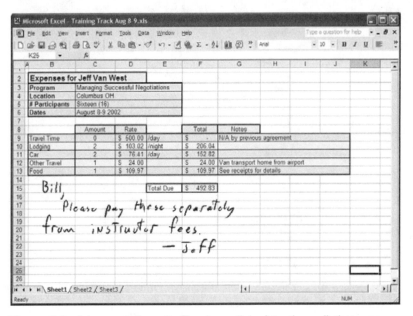

Figure 8-2   Ink annotations in Excel are linked to the cell that was selected when they were created.

Microsoft Office PowerPoint 2003 Annotations

Ink might seem like an intuitive feature in PowerPoint; in fact, the Pen option has been around in PowerPoint for several generations. Ink is helpful in presentations for drawing circles and arrows on slides; and it can be a dramatic addition to a slide showing a table, diagram, or chart. In fact, in PowerPoint 2003, you can create entirely hand-drawn slides, if that meets your presentation needs.

Ink in Microsoft Office Outlook 2003

Finally, ink in Outlook enables you to write out your e-mail messages long-hand, draw maps to the downtown bookstore, sign your name with a real signature, or make notes on an e-mail message you're forwarding. Additionally, you can write out your to-do list, add the items to your task view, and create Calendar entries using ink.

Internet Faxing

Office 2003 builds in the option of using an Internet service to send a fax from within Word, Excel, or PowerPoint. Relying on partnerships in the Microsoft Office Marketplace, Office enables you to choose Sent to in the File menu and select the new Fax Service option. (See Figure 8-3.)

Figure 8-3   Internet fax capability is now built into Word, Excel, and PowerPoint.

The first time you choose the Fax Service option, a prompt lets you know that you need to sign up for an Internet fax service. When you click OK, you are taken to the Office Marketplace Web site, where you can choose a fax service provider. After that, you'll be able to send and receive faxes automatically while you work in your favorite applications.

IRM (Information Rights Management)

IRM technology is a new addition to Office 2003 that enables you to limit others' accessibility to your critical business documents. IRM actually protects the document at a file level (as opposed to the network level), giving users controls that can allow or disable features that could be used to forward materials to people outside the organization or change valuable data that shouldn't be modified.

IRM: Quick Facts

Here's a quick look at some of the key features of IRM:

- A document-protection model that works at the file level.

- Features for protected documents can be disabled to block forwarding, e-mailing, faxing, printing, or editing.

- Users can set expiration dates for documents so that they will not be viewable past a certain date.

- Microsoft offers an IRM Viewer free of charge to organizations receiving IRM-protected documents that do not currently use Office 2003.

- IRM requires Windows .NET Server and a premium Client Access License.

All businesses have sensitive data that they want to ensure stays within the limits of the organization. Payroll information, private personnel data, critical strategic information, specifications for new products, and valuable market research are just a few of the documents organizations want to keep a handle on. By using the IRM features in Office 2003, organizations can limit how far a document can travel and control what can be done with it. For example, the forwarding, copying, and printing features might be disabled for a sensitive e-mail message; attached documents are similarly protected.

In Word and Excel, users are assigned various roles, depending on the level of permission they are granted in a specific document. A Viewer can view files as read-only and cannot make any modifications; Reviewer enables a user to make comments in a file and add information; Editor grants editing privileges so that the file can be modified.

Tip   This assignment of roles is a feature IRM has in common with SharePoint Team Services, which enables you to grant various levels of access to SharePoint Team Services sites by choosing Reader, Contributor, Web Designer, or Administrator roles for team members.

Research Task Pane

The new Research task pane is another sophisticated feature in Office 2003 that enables information workers to bring additional resources to their current applications. The Research task pane enables users to search for information on the company intranet, over the Internet, or in a variety of sources both inside and outside their regular applications. This enables them to find the information they need—a word, a definition, a translation—on the fly, without stopping work in their current document.

Built into the Research task pane is an extensive Research Library that houses a number of resources, including a multilanguage thesaurus and dictionaries, an automatic translation utility, and an Internet encyclopedia. Users can also subscribe to third-party resource providers, which can be added to the Research options and searched automatically.

Users can display the task pane in the usual way—by choosing View, Task Pane and then selecting Research from the drop-down list in the upper-right corner of the task bar, but there's also a more intuitive way. When a user wants to find out more about a specific word, the user can hold the Alt key and click the word; the Research utility does a quick search and displays alternate definitions (as well as antonyms, synonyms, and more) in the Research task pane. (See Figure 8-4, on the next page.)

Figure 8-4   The Research task pane searches the Research Library sources and displays options for the selected word.

From the Experts

Mark Dodge, coauthor of *Microsoft Office Excel 2003 Inside Out* (Microsoft Press, 2003), says: "I think one of the coolest things in Office—and it's not an often talked-about feature—is the translation capability. You can enter a word and get a translation immediately in any language you select." The Translation feature is available when you scroll through the resources in the Research task pane.

Picture Library

The new Microsoft Picture Library gives you image-editing tools when you work with Picture Libraries on SharePoint Team Services sites. When you or your team members create picture libraries, you can upload images from your local hard drives or network drives; import images from digital cameras or scanners; and post images to the team site.

When you click an image in a picture library and then click the Edit Picture tool, the Microsoft Picture Library opens. (See Figure 8-5.) This utility enables you to perform basic image-editing functions on the selected picture. These editing possibilities include the following:

- Change brightness and contrast
- Alter the color of the picture
- Crop the image
- Rotate and flip the image
- Remove red eye in the photo
- Resize the picture

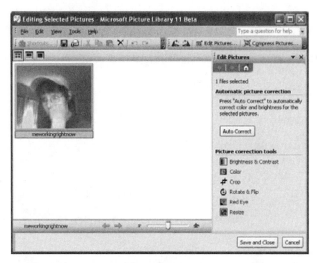

Figure 8-5   The Microsoft Picture Library is a new tool in Office 2003 that enables you to edit your pictures.

> **Tip** The easiest modification is the one to try first: click AutoCorrect to cause the Picture Library to correct the color and brightness of the selected image for the best possible display.

You can also use the Microsoft Picture Library to print pictures; export images to other file formats; e-mail pictures to friends and coworkers; compress images; and work with images in groups for export, conversion, or print processes.

Word 2003 Enhancements

Like all Office applications, the look of Word 2003 has changed to match the Microsoft Windows XP theme and style. The biggest change in Word is the XML support (ability to create XML files, apply XML tags, and attach XML schema), but a number of other enhancement features give you more flexibility in the way you work with and secure Word documents.

> **More Info** For more about working with XML in the various Office applications, see Chapter 5, "Support for XML."

Reading Layout Mode

The second-biggest change in Word's appearance is in the addition of a new view: Reading Layout mode. This view was created to allow users to read and navigate through a document without needing to print it out. Users can switch easily to Reading Layout mode anytime they're viewing a document by clicking the Start Reading tool in the Standard toolbar.

Figure 8-6 shows the Reading Layout view. By default, the current page is displayed in full-page view in the reading pane on the right side of the screen; thumbnails of additional pages are displayed in the left column.

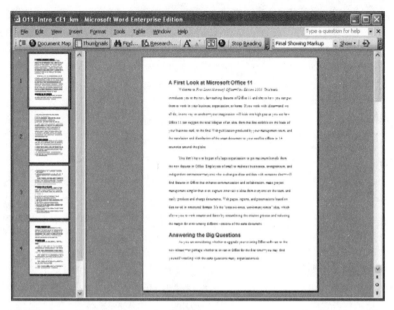

Figure 8-6 Reading Layout mode enables users to read a document in a way that is similar to reading a book.

Enhancing Reading

At first glance, the document in the Reading Layout pane might not be readable—the text might be too small. You can enlarge the text in two ways: by clicking the Increase Text Size tool to make the document text larger (you can click the tool several times to increase text size continually), or by clicking Actual Size to toggle between the default size and the most recently used Increased Text Size value you selected.

> **Tip** If you want to scan through a document quickly to locate tables, charts, or simply to check the overall layout of the document, you can display the document in two-page view in Reading Layout mode.

Navigating Reading Layout

By default, Reading Layout mode displays thumbnail views along the left side of the Word window, but you can replace the thumbnails with the Word Document Map if you want to use it to move to specific sections in your document. Simply click the Document Map tool in the Reading Layout toolbar, and the map appears. You can then move directly to the section you want to see by clicking the appropriate section title.

Style Locking

Now in Word 2003, you can set your styles in stone with style locking. This feature enables you to limit what other users can do in your document and block their attempts at boldfacing, italicizing, or reformatting parts of a collaborative document. By locking the styles used in the document, you hold other users to sticking with those particular styles—and nothing more.

To enable style locking, you work in the Document Protection task pane (displayed by choosing Protect Document from the Tools menu) and click the Limit Formatting To A Selection Of Styles check box. When you click Settings, the Formatting Restrictions dialog box appears, enabling you to choose the styles you want to allow in the document. (See Figure 8-7.)

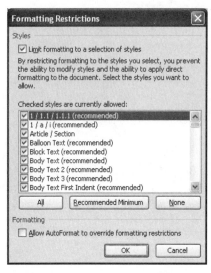

Figure 8-7   You can use style locking to prohibit other users from adding formatting changes.

> **Tip**   Click the Recommended Minimum button if you want Word to set the suggested minimum number of allowable styles for the document.

Editing Restrictions

A second protection feature is included in the Document Protection task pane. By setting Editing restrictions in a document, you can limit the types of changes that users are allowed to make.

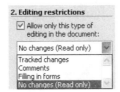

Allowing Changes in Document Sections

Yet another protection feature (also in the Document Protection task pane) enables you to allow selected users to make changes in specific parts of a document. For example, suppose that you're preparing a draft of a report that includes input from Sales, Marketing, and Distribution departments. When you send the document to someone in charge of the sales information, you can permit edits only in that user's section of the document. When you send the document to Marketing for review, you can allow edits in the marketing section, and so on.

Excel 2003 Enhancements

The biggest changes to Excel include the addition of powerful XML support features, linking to XML schema, transforms upon Open and Save, and the drag-and-drop visual mapping capability for building XML documents in Excel. Additionally, other enhancements we've already covered—such as Tablet PC ink support and the new Research task pane—make Excel more flexible and easier to use.

Links to SharePoint Team Services

Another significant enhancement in Excel includes its seamless integration with SharePoint Team Services. Now you can import SharePoint list data directly into your Excel spreadsheet, and export that data back to SharePoint just as easily. The Datasheet view in your SharePoint Team Services site provides the tools you'll use to work seamlessly with Excel. (See Figure 8-8.)

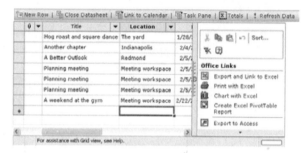

Figure 8-8 You can import and export Excel data to and from SharePoint Team Services sites.

Additional improvements in Excel have been made in the enhanced smart tag functionality and in the number of statistical functions currently supported.

From the Experts

Craig Stinson, coauthor of *Microsoft Office Excel 2003 Inside Out* (Microsoft Press, 2003), says: "List management is something a large number of spreadsheet people do in Excel...phone lists, contact lists, grocery lists...because it's so easy to do. The list-management features, and the integration with SharePoint Team Services, will make a huge difference. People will use those features. And what will really make a difference is seeing XML in larger adoption."

PowerPoint Enhancements

Many PowerPoint additions in Office 2003 have been discussed earlier. PowerPoint's additions include the Research task pane (already covered in this chapter), which enables you to find out more about a subject or phrase used in your presentation; the Shared Workspace (Chapter 3) allows you and other team members to work collaboratively on a presentation using SharePoint Team Services. Smart tag functionality (Chapter 6) appears for the first time in PowerPoint 2003.

This section introduces you to new features in PowerPoint 2003 not covered elsewhere in the book. These items include the new Package To CD option, slide show annotations, enhanced integration with Microsoft Windows Media Player, and the option of showing full-screen movie clips during a presentation rather than limiting them to a small display box.

> Tip   In addition to the Research task pane shared with other Office 2003 applications, PowerPoint has its own Thesaurus Dialog option (in the Tools menu). To do a quick check on a word, highlight the word and press Shift+F7. PowerPoint does a quick lookup and displays alternate words in the Thesaurus section of the Research task pane.

Packaging Presentations

Specific changes to the program include the replacement of the Pack and Go Wizard with the Package to CD option. This feature enables you to prepare your presentation and burn it to a CD that can be run on another user's system, even if that user doesn't have PowerPoint. The Package for CD dialog box enables you to name the CD and add files as needed. (See Figure 8-9, on the next page.) When you click the Copy to CD button, PowerPoint copies the files quickly to the CD and then ejects it and asks whether you want to copy the same presentation files to another CD.

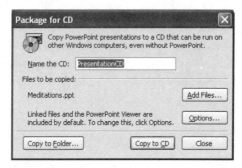

Figure 8-9 The Package for CD option allows you to copy your presentation easily to a CD and include all necessary files.

> **Tip** When you are packaging the presentation, you can click Options to specify how you want the CD to play the presentations. You can also password-protect the presentation.

Slide Show Annotations

New ink support in PowerPoint 2003 enables presenters to add handwritten notes on slides during the presentation or save annotations to slides for later display. An improved presentation toolbar gives you a new way to display pen options. (See Figure 8-10.) Now you can choose your tool (arrow, ballpoint pen, felt tip pen, or highlighter), select an ink color, and you're good to go.

Figure 8-10 You can choose a tool to make annotations during a presentation.

Improved Navigation Tools

The slide show toolbar has been improved in other ways, as well. The Slide Navigator has been replaced with a button that displays only navigation-related options. You can move easily to a specific slide by choosing it from the Go To Slide submenu; you can pause the presentation and go to a black or white screen while you have a discussion. You can still display the Speaker Notes dialog box to add specific comments, questions, or items you want to look up later. (See Figure 8-11.)

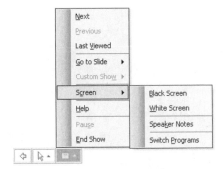

Figure 8-11   The improved navigation controls are easier to use and make more options available to you while you're presenting.

A new option in the Screen submenu, Switch Programs, displays the Windows Taskbar so that you can easily display another program you might have waiting in the wings. For example, suppose that you are giving a presentation that introduces a new product to your regional sales managers. Before the presentation, you opened an Excel worksheet showing sales projections for the product, but you minimized it so that you can use it only if you need to. When one of the regional managers asks a question about sales projections, you can choose Switch Programs, click the Excel icon in the Taskbar, and display and discuss the projections before returning to your presentation.

Full-Screen Movie Playback

In previous versions of PowerPoint, movie objects played in a small rectangular area on the presentation slide. In PowerPoint 2003, you have the option of maximizing the movie so that it plays in full-screen view. This allows you to launch a short video of a new product or an interview with the product designer, run it full-screen, and then return seamlessly to the presentation. The option for playing a movie in full-screen view is available in the Movie Options dialog box. (See Figure 8-12.)

Figure 8-12   PowerPoint 2003 enables you to play a movie clip in full-screen view.

Microsoft Office Access 2003 Enhancements

The big improvement in Access is XML support built into the easy import and export capabilities of the program. As explained in Chapter 5, XML support makes it possible for Access to work with virtually any kind of file (given the necessary transforms). The additional enhancements in Access have to do with simplifying complicated tasks and making things easier for users and developers. This section gives you a quick look at the productivity enhancements in Access.

Smart Tags Identifying Common Errors

Access 2003 puts smart tag technology to work by using it to help let users know about common errors that occur in Access databases. For example, when Access encounters an invalid control source or an unassociated label, a smart tag indicator underlines the item. When the user positions the pointer over the item, the smart tag icon appears; by clicking it, the user will see a list of possible actions for identifying and resolving the error.

> **Tip**   Access also supports the use of the AutoCorrect smart tag for common data-entry errors, such as incorrect capitalization, and can expedite text entry by replacing the abbreviated text a user types with the longer company or product name, for example.

Creating a Backup Database

Now Access 2003 can easily create a backup copy of important database files by using the Back Up Database command directly from Access's File menu. When you choose the command, Access displays the Save Backup As dialog box and names the database file with the current date so that future backups do not overwrite previous versions. (See Figure 8-13.)

Figure 8-13   The new Back Up Database option enables you to easily create a backup of important files.

Identifying Dependencies

When you rename or revise database objects, it's easy to forget—especially in a complicated database system—the variety of items that depend on that particular item. Access 2003 includes an Object Dependencies command that enables you to find out which other objects (tables, forms, queries, and reports) depend on the item you are modifying. You can evaluate dependencies by right-clicking the object and choosing Object Dependencies, as you can see in Figure 8-14. The Object Dependencies task pane shows you the objects that will be affected. When you make the change, the objects are updated automatically for you.

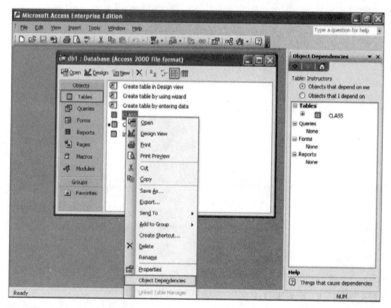

Figure 8-14   Access 2003 shows you the objects that depend on the selected item.

Simplified Copying of Linked Tables

In previous versions of Access, the steps involved in copying a linked table to your local database were complicated; now the process is simplified so that you can copy a linked table to your local database using a simple copy-and-paste procedure. Additionally, a link appears in the Access task pane as a common action under Linked Tables.

Microsoft Office FrontPage 2003 Improvements

FrontPage 2003 includes so many improvements and enhancements that we'd need an entire chapter just to go through them all. Generally, the major changes include advances in the following areas:

- New and expanded coding features to make working with code much easier

- HTML authoring and cleanup features

- A great new editor with many new tools and views

- Direct text-file editing

- The ability to work with a larger number of source types and display using a wider range of browsers

- The option of previewing in multiple browsers

- Design changes to make formatting tables and Web Parts easier

- Integration with SharePoint Team Services to publish Web components and work seamlessly with SharePoint data lists and libraries

- Support for ASP.NET and script authoring

- Publishing to FTP and WebDAV servers

- A new data source catalog that enables you to add data views from SharePoint Team Services, XML, Web services, or Microsoft SQL Server

- A Web Part Gallery

- Integration with Microsoft Picture Library for simple image-editing tasks

---

Tip   The changes in FrontPage are substantial and could fill a book on their own. In fact, they do! See Jim Buyens's *Microsoft Office FrontPage 2003 Inside Out* (Microsoft Press, 2003), for more information.

New Look for FrontPage

FrontPage 2003 has a new layout for the main work window. (See Figure 8-15.) Now the navigation bar along the left of the window is gone, giving you more room on-screen, along with four view buttons (Design, Split, Code, and Preview) that enable you to move easily among perspectives.

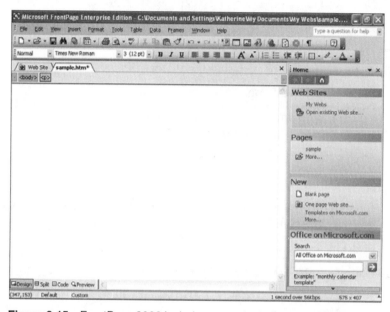

Figure 8-15   FrontPage 2003 includes a new look that makes better use of screen space and provides more tools within reach of the mouse.

New Views

The Split pane is an addition that enables you to see Design and Code views simultaneously. Also, line numbers are now displayed in Code (formerly HTML) view. A new Quick Tag toolbar gives you information about the tags used on the current line. (See Figure 8-16.)

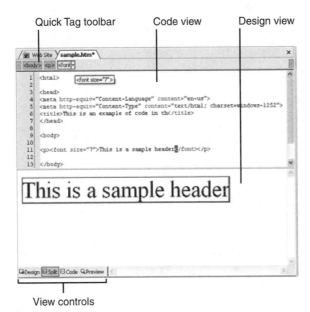

Figure 8-16   New views in FrontPage enable you to see the effects of your work and make changes accordingly with help from the new Tag toolbar.

> **Tip**   FrontPage 2003 also includes a new Remote Site view that enables you to see and transfer files among local and remote Web sites.

Table Layout Controls

FrontPage 2003 makes it easy to create tables of all kinds and add special effects, including rounded corners, borders, and shadows to individual cells. Using the Layout Tables And Cells task pane, you can create a layout table or choose settings for the entire table or individual cells.

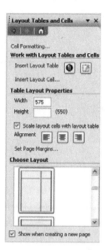

New Browser Options

FrontPage 2003 allows you to preview your pages in a specific browser or in a number of different browsers. You can select the browser size and even display the same page in multiple browsers simultaneously.

From the Experts

Jim Buyens, author of *Microsoft Office FrontPage 2003 Inside Out,* thinks the dynamic templates feature will be a big help to users. He says, "...if I make a template for a Web page...I set up the background picture and set my text colors and put a header and footer on the page...I can then designate one or more areas on the page as editable, which means that the page that uses the template can put variable content in there. From there, you can open other Web pages and attach that template to them. The page template features—with the non-editable background, header, footer, and copyright information—appear on the page, with the customizable content in the middle." This could be deployed to many different sites, across an organization. But now suppose I go back and change the template. FrontPage can now go out, find, and change all linked pages, so the template changes are made to all linked sites immediately with no effect on the content.

Microsoft Office Document Imaging

Microsoft Office Document Imaging, which is available with Microsoft Office Tools in the All Programs submenu, has gone through a significant growth spurt. Now the utility includes three toolbars instead of one (Views, Annotate, and Standard); offers improvements in OCR (optical character recognition) technology; provides a search feature; and allows annotations on the documents you scan, convert, and use. (See Figure 8-17.)

Figure 8-17   Microsoft Office Document Imaging includes a number of enhancements, including an annotations feature to support ink capability throughout Office 2003.

Microsoft Office 2003 Outlook with Business Contact Manager

Microsoft Office 2003 Outlook with Business Contact Manager is a new utility that helps owners of small businesses keep track of valuable data in the form of contacts, leads, and customer information. This Outlook add-on provides a simple contact manager with the familiar Outlook interface, enabling users to manage their customer information; track appointments and tasks; collect documents, photos, and more; manage follow-up actions; and report on the status of customer relationships.

Summary

This chapter has given you a quick look at the many enhancements in the various applications in Office 2003. From the Office-wide addition of ink and Tablet PC support to IRM (Information Rights Management) to the individual enhancements in each of the core Office 2003 programs, the changes throughout Office are designed to help you work however is best for you. The streamlined procedures, flexible data formats, improved tools, and seamless integration with Web services and XML-based technologies throughout Office will enable you to expand the effective use of your data, throughout your department or across your enterprise.

Resources

Because Microsoft Office 2003 is still an emerging topic, resources for finding out more about it are a bit limited in number. This appendix provides you with links and references you can consult to learn more about the various aspects and applications of Office 2003. The listings are divided into the following categories:

- General Office Resources
- Office Developer Resources
- XML Resources
- Microsoft Office 2003 Applications

General Office Resources

- *Tablet PC Quick Reference*, by Jeff Van West (Microsoft Press, 2003). A full look at the range of features available on your Tablet PC that shows you how to use your Tablet with Office applications.
- Microsoft Office 2003: *www.betanews.com*
- "Microsoft Office 11 Preview," Paul Thurrott, *SuperSite for Windows*, Dec. 6, 2002: *www.winsupersite.com/reviews/office11_beta1.asp*
- "Microsoft's Next Office: More Than Meets the Eye," Yardena Arar, *PC World*, Jan. 2003: *www.pcworld.com/news/article/0,aid,107486,00.asp*

Office Developer Resources

- *Programming Microsoft Visual Basic .NET*, by Francesco Balena (Microsoft Press, 2002). A book for developers and solution-providers that answers questions about Visual Basic .NET and supplies many real-world code examples.
- Microsoft Developer Network: *www.msdn.microsoft.com/office*

- Developing Simple Smart Tags: *msdn.microsoft.com/library/en-us/dnsmarttag/html/odc_stxml.asp*

- Developing Smart Tag DLLs: *msdn.microsoft.com/library/en-us/dnsmarttag/html/odc_smarttags.asp*

- Smart Tag SDK 1.1: *msdn.microsoft.com/library/en-us/dnsmarttag/html/odc_smarttags.asp*

- Smart Tag Enterprise Resource Kit: *msdn.microsoft.com/downloads/default.asp?url=/downloads/sample.asp?url=/msdn-files/027/001/835/msdncompositedoc.xml*

- Office 2003 for Developers: *www.microsoft.com/office/developer/preview/*

- "Microsoft Office 11, An App Platform," by Thor Olavsrud. Developer, Dec. 9, 2002: *www.internetnews.com/dev-news/article.php/1553991*

- "New Development Tools to Accompany Office 11," *Advisor*, Dec. 11, 2002: *www.advisor.com/doc/11582*

- "What's New in Smart Tags in Office 11," MSDN Microsoft Web site: *www.microsoft.com/columns/office.asp*

- "Office 11 Programming Suite Touted," Paul Thurrott, *Wininfo*, Dec. 10, 2002: *www.wininformant.com/Articles/Index.ctm?ArticleID=27539*

- Microsoft TechNet (for IT professionals): *www.microsoft.com/technet/*

- Microsoft .NET: *www.microsoft.com/net/*

XML Resources

- *XML Step by Step, Second Edition*, by Michael J. Young (Microsoft Press, 2002). This book teaches you how to understand and apply the latest XML technology and standards. A great companion book for those who want to take full advantage of the widespread XML support in Office 2003.

- For additional information on the W3C XML specification and Microsoft's implementation of XML, visit *msdn.microsoft.com/xml/*.

- For additional information on new solution capabilities in Office 2003, visit *www.microsoft.com/office/developer/preview/*.

- Article with Jean Paoli on the XML support in Office 2003: *www.infoworld.com/articles/op/xml/02/11/14/021114opwebserv.xml*

- "Microsoft Readies XML Editor," by Matt Berger, IDG News Service, Oct. 9, 2002: *www.pcworld.com/news/article/0,aid,105762.asp*

- "Microsoft Office 11 and InfoPath [XDocs]," Cover Pages, Feb. 10, 2003: *www.xml.coverpages.org/microsoftXDocs.html*

- Microsoft Office InfoPath 2003 Web site: *www.microsoft.com/office/preview/infopath*

- World Wide Web Consortium: *www.w3.org*

Microsoft Office 2003 Application Resources

These new books, available soon from Microsoft Press, will help you learn more about the various offerings in Office 2003. To find out about book availability, visit Microsoft Press online at *www.microsoft.com/mpress/*.

- *Introducing Microsoft Office 2003 InfoPath*, by Acey Bunch (Microsoft Press, 2003). Learn about this new native-XML tool and discover how to develop InfoPath solutions for your organization.

- *Microsoft Office Professional Edition 2003 Inside Out*, by Michael J. Young (Microsoft Press, 2003). Use this comprehensive reference to explore each of the core Office 2003 applications in depth and find out how you can make the most of the enhanced collaboration and communication features in this release.

- *Microsoft Office Excel 2003 Inside Out*, by Mark Dodge and Craig Stinson (Microsoft Press, 2003). Find expert information on using Excel 2003 and develop sophisticated Excel worksheets using the newest features.

- *Microsoft Office FrontPage 2003 Inside Out*, by Jim Buyens (Microsoft Press, 2003). Get the latest-and-greatest ideas on using FrontPage 2003 for high-level site design and publishing.

■   *Microsoft Office Outlook 2003 Inside Out*, by Jim Boyce (Microsoft Press, 2003). Learn more about the many changes in Outlook 2003 and find out how you can use the new features to better organize the way you work with groups and individuals.

■   *Microsoft Office Word 2003 Inside Out*, by Mary Millhollon and Katherine Murray (Microsoft Press, 2003). Explore Word 2003 as a super-user and put the XML and shared workspace features of Office 2003 to work as you create professional documents that can be shared, stored, published, and used as your business needs dictate.

Katherine Murray

Katherine Murray is also the author of *Faster, Smarter Microsoft Office XP* (Microsoft Press, 2002) and coauthor of *Microsoft Word Version 2002 Inside Out* (Microsoft Press, 2001). She has written more than 40 computer books (and a number of parenting books) on topics ranging from general computer use to more specialized books on presentation graphics, Internet use, and Web animation. For the last 15 years, Katherine has owned and operated reVisions Plus, Inc., a writing and publishing services company that relies primarily on Office applications. She also writes how-to articles for the Microsoft Office Community (www.microsoft.com/office/) and publishes an online journal for Microsoft Office users, called BlogofficeXP.

W. Frederick Zimmerman

W. Frederick Zimmerman writes, speaks and consults for OneNoteInfo-Center.com, an independent resource for users of Microsoft Office OneNote 2003. Previously, he directed energy technology strategy for LexisNexis. He lives in Ann Arbor, Michigan with his wife Cheryl and his children Kelsey and Parker.

Brian Johnson

Brian Johnson is a programming editor at Microsoft. He lives in Redmond, Washington with his wife Kathy, and their three children, Will, Hunter, and Buffy. Brian is a coauthor of *Inside Visual Studio .NET 2003* also published by Microsoft Press (2003).

Colophon

The manuscript for this book was prepared and galleyed using Microsoft Word. Pages were composed by Studioserv (www.studioserv.com) using Adobe FrameMaker for Windows, with text in Garamond and display type in Helvetica Condensed Black. Composed pages were delivered to the printer as electronic prepress files.

Cover Designer: Patricia Bradbury
Interior Graphic Designer: James D. Kramer
Principal Compositor: Sharon Bell
Copy Editor: Teri Kieffer
Indexer: Julie Kawabata

Index

Work smarter—*conquer your software from the inside out!*

Microsoft® Windows® XP Inside Out, Deluxe Edition
ISBN: 0-7356-1805-4
U.S.A.　$59.99
Canada　$86.99

Microsoft Office XP Inside Out
ISBN: 0-7356-1277-3
U.S.A.　$44.99
Canada　$64.99

Microsoft Access Version 2002 Inside Out
ISBN: 0-7356-1283-8
U.S.A.　$44.99
Canada　$64.99

Microsoft FrontPage® Version 2002 Inside Out
ISBN: 0-7356-1284-6
U.S.A.　$44.99
Canada　$64.99

Hey, you know your way around a desktop. Now dig into Office XP applications and the Windows XP operating system and *really* put your PC to work! These supremely organized software reference titles pack hundreds of timesaving solutions, troubleshooting tips and tricks, and handy workarounds into a concise, fast-answer format. They're all muscle and no fluff. All this comprehensive information goes deep into the nooks and crannies of each Office application and Windows XP feature. And every INSIDE OUT title includes a CD-ROM packed with bonus content such as tools and utilities, demo programs, sample scripts, batch programs, an eBook containing the book's complete text, and more! Discover the best and fastest ways to perform everyday tasks, and challenge yourself to new levels of software mastery!

Microsoft Press has other INSIDE OUT titles to help you get the job done every day:

Microsoft Office Version X for Mac Inside Out
ISBN: 0-7356-1628-0

Microsoft Word Version 2002 Inside Out
ISBN: 0-7356-1278-1

Microsoft Excel Version 2002 Inside Out
ISBN: 0-7356-1281-1

Microsoft Outlook Version 2002 Inside Out
ISBN: 0-7356-1282-X

Microsoft Project Version 2002 Inside Out
ISBN: 0-7356-1124-6

Microsoft Visio® Version 2002 Inside Out
ISBN: 0-7356-1285-4

Microsoft Windows XP Networking Inside Out
ISBN: 0-7356-1652-3

Microsoft Windows Security Inside Out for Windows XP and Windows 2000
ISBN: 0-7356-1632-9

To learn more about the full line of Microsoft Press® products, please visit us at:

microsoft.com/mspress

Get a **Free**
e-mail newsletter, updates,
special offers, links to related books,
and more when you

register on line!

Register your Microsoft Press® title on our Web site and you'll get
a FREE subscription to our e-mail newsletter, *Microsoft Press Book
Connections.* You'll find out about newly released and upcoming books
and learning tools, online events, software downloads, special offers
and coupons for Microsoft Press customers, and information about
major Microsoft® product releases. You can also read useful additional
information about all the titles we publish, such as detailed book
descriptions, tables of contents and indexes, sample chapters, links to
related books and book series, author biographies, and reviews by other
customers.

Registration is easy. Just visit this Web page and fill in your information:

http://www.microsoft.com/mspress/register

Microsoft®

Proof of Purchase

Use this page as proof of purchase if participating in a promotion or rebate offer on
this title. Proof of purchase must be used in conjunction with other proof(s) of
payment such as your dated sales receipt—see offer details.

First Look Microsoft® Office Professional Edition 2003
0-7356-1951-4

CUSTOMER NAME

Microsoft Press, PO Box 97017, Redmond, WA 98073-9830